P9-AOW-985

Manual #1 in the
Working With Diversity Series

Learning Styles and Strategies

3rd Edition, 1998

WHO AM I AS A: **LEARNER?**
                        TEACHER?

WHAT ARE MY: **ASSETS?**
                        LIABILITIES?

HOW CAN I WORK MORE EFFECTIVELY WITH:
             STUDENTS?   **PARENTS?**
             TEACHERS?   **ADMINISTRATORS?**

By

J. Robert Hanson and Harvey F. Silver

Published by

The Thoughtful Education Press
a division of
Silver Strong & Associates, Inc.
Crestwood Professional Building, Suite #23
941 Whitehorse Avenue
Trenton, NJ 08610
800-962-4432
www.silverstrong.com

ISBN# 1-58284-001-6

ACKNOWLEDGEMENTS

The authors wish to express their thanks to the many teachers and administrators across the country who shared their ideas and criticisms with us, and who provided a lively laboratory for the testing and refining of these ideas and activities.

The authors also wish to acknowledge the many Jungian scholars and the personnel from the Center for the Application of Personality Type in Florida who both stimulated the writing of the manual, and who shared their insights and enthusiasms with us.

Finally, we want to invite your comments, commendations and recommendations to this manual so that it may be continually improved to better serve the needs of teachers.

J. Robert Hanson   Harvey F. Silver
119 Mt. Laurel Rd.   434 Heights Rd.
Moorestown, NJ 08057   Ridgewood, NJ 07450

February, 1996

DEDICATION

The manual, and the series from which it comes, is dedicated to all those teachers who knew, by instinct or experience, that every child learned differently, had preferences different from their own, needed "space" to be what s/he could become, and gave that child approval and encouragement in the process.

The manual is also dedicated to those individuals, teachers or otherwise, who seek an increased awareness of how they function as learners, who have the courage to become the best that they may be, and in the process of becoming radiate humor and a zest for living. May they end up in our nation's classrooms.

TABLE OF CONTENTS

1

CHAPTER ONE

Working Constructively With Diversity

Introduction

During the past twenty years our understanding of individual differences has become richer and deeper. Yet the widespread recognition that students learn in different ways and have different needs has not been satisfactorily accompanied by the development of teacher knowledge and skills in recognizing and dealing with these diversities. If teachers are to read and to respond to the messages of behavioral diversity they must first be provided with the training, materials, and resources needed to achieve these goals.

The purpose of this manual is to assist classroom teachers in diagnosing learning styles and profiles, and in assimilating the knowledge, skills and attitudes necessary to more effectively read and respond to students' needs.

Unlike books that can be read somewhat passively this one requires interaction with the text, the actual doing of the proposed exercises, the completion of the diagnostic instruments, and the answering of the self-analysis questions. Above and beyond the actual doing of the manual our hope is that you will think about what these procedures mean for your own life and for your teaching.

What Kids Need

Faculty lounges are often the arenas for debates on what kids need. In a teachers' lounge we might hear these comments: One teacher, an ex-military man, comes into the lounge after just having marked a weekly quiz. He is visibly upset. He appears uncomfortable in his starched collar and precisely knotted tie. "What these kids need," he says, "is more discipline and hard work. They need to pay more attention to learning the basic skills."

A second teacher disagrees. As she speaks she waters a bedraggled plant. "What kids need," she says, "is understanding, a little love and affection, or at least the knowledge that teachers like and care about them as individuals. Children need to know that teachers can be trusted, and that teachers have some understanding of their personal problems. We need to help our kids develop a strong self-concept and learn how to get along with others."

A third teacher agrees that kids need to learn to work hard, and that, of course, love, understanding, and a strong self-concept are important. As he fills his pipe and searches in his tweed jacket for matches, he says, "What these kids really need is intellectual stimulation. They need to learn to think for themselves. They need to be challenged to see meanings, possibilities and relationships among ideas. They need to learn to ask 'why?'"

The fourth teacher sits quietly through the discussion. From his paint-spattered shirt it is apparent that he teaches in one of the arts. "What kids need," he says, "is the opportunity to be creative, to explore their minds, to use their imaginations, to discover their unique potentials, and to examine their own values."[1]

What do kids really need? Is it hard work and skills mastery, love and affection, intellectual challenge, or the opportunity to explore their creative abilities? The question is: "Who's right?" or "Are they all partially right?"

This debate on the question of "who's right?" reminds us of the story of the six blind men who were invited to the Raja's palace to learn about the elephant. Each blind man, examining a different part of the elephant, came up with a different definition of the animal. Each blind man was insistent that his experience of the elephant was definitive. Hence, the elephant was like, in turn, a rope, a snake, a tree trunk, a wall, a spear, etc. According to the story, a vigorous argument ensued until the Rajah intervened to explain that they were all both right and wrong. The elephant was, in fact, all the experiences and more. The story of the six blind men and the elephant survives as a classic because it describes a universal human condition, i.e., that we assume that our own experiences are definitive until challenged to look further.

As the wise Rajah explained to the blind men that they were all both right and wrong an important truth was revealed. This truth says that partial knowledge is inherently incomplete and therefore probably inaccurate. How we experience a student should, likewise, not be assumed to be definitive until we've learned a lot more both about him, and about ourselves. To deal with the human psyche is to deal with immense diversity. This diversity is twice compounded: once by the student being viewed, and once again by the viewer. Blindness, or sight, is in the eye of the beholder.

Working With Diversity: The Versus Issue

We also believe that these stories illustrate an important dilemma in which we, and our students, find ourselves. This is the "versus" issue. Education has been compared to a beach where each breaking wave represents a different instructional emphasis. There is open classroom versus traditional classroom; basic skills versus affective education; teacher-directed learning versus student-directed learning; individualized instruction versus large group instruction; modern math versus traditional math; behavior modification versus values clarification, and so on. We are like pebbles washed up and down the beach as each educational emphasis ebbs and flows. The

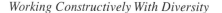

versus issues represent important emphases in learning that are always present. What is clearly needed is a way to put each set of polarities into a more meaningful context. In short, what we need is a way to take the emphasis out the arena of competition and to put the polarities within a framework where each is seen as essential content for developing programs responsive to the diverse needs of individual learners.

Working With Diversity: The Dualities Within Us

The versus issue can also be seen within each individual as a set of dualities in dynamic tension. The dualities within us include both cosmic and psychic forces, and both are at work simultaneously, the one affecting the other in myriad combinations. We are, for example, both child and adult, male and female, brave and fearful, open and hidden, articulate and confused, caring and apathetic, reflective and impulsive. Both sides of these dualities are present in all of us. Because of constitutional determinants, spontaneous initial preferences, environmental influences, and societal pressures, we develop a preference for one side of the duality over the other. These preferences, even when we are not aware of them, have continued impact on the decisions we make and the way we behave. These dualities affect our teaching and learning as well. We are, for example, both process and product oriented; objective and subjective, analytical and personal; garrulous and reticent, concrete and abstract. Our personality evolves as we exercise preferences and begin to trust one side of the duality over the other.

A simple yet dramatic way to demonstrate how preferences for one side of a duality affect behavior is as follows:

LEARNING PREFERENCE EXPERIMENT

Please follow the directions exactly as written.

Step #1. In 15 seconds, write your name, address and telephone number on a piece of paper.

Step #2. Now turn the paper upside down, and follow the instructions.

Using the opposite hand write your name, address and telephone number. Do this in 15 seconds.

Step #3. Answer the following questions:

• What were your feelings when using the preferred hand?

_____

• How did the second writing compare to the first in legibility, neatness, etc.? Were you able to complete the assignment with the second hand within the 15 seconds allotted?

_____

_____

• What does this experiment suggest in terms of preferences and dualities?

_____

_____

As we choose one hand over the other a dominance is determined which leads to greater skill with and trust for the preferred hand. By the same token, the opposite hand's development is generally retarded or arrested. This process is also true for the other dualities within us. The choice of one polarity or preference over another leads to greater skill and dependence. Simultaneously, the ignored function or behavior, like an unused or less used muscle, becomes less developed and hence less reliable.

The choice of behavioral preferences is far more subtle than is the choice of one hand over another. We are sometimes unaware of our own preferences, or why one side of the duality is chosen over its opposite. As an example, we have all experienced the frustration of not knowing what choices to make, or of feeling the contradiction between what we want and what we choose. These choices may be the result of the tension we feel between our concept of what we are contrasted with what we'd like to become, or our self-expectations versus the expectations of the institutions we serve, e.g., family, school, or job.

Working With Diversity: The Dualities Between Us

The dualities within us are matched by a large number of dualities or preferences between us. As teachers we need to be able to recognize and deal with such differences as those between the convergent and divergent thinkers, those who abstract and those who concretize, the introvert and the extravert, those who are field dependent and those who are field independent, and contextual versus detail preferences.

The interactions between these dualities are often implicit in the questions teachers ask themselves about their students, e.g.:

- Why is it that I work more effectively with one student than another?

- Why does one activity interest a particular student while another fails to stimulate interest?

- Why does one child work well independently while another needs a great deal of assistance?

- Why does one child like to work alone while another prefers group activities?

- Why must one child work to have everything correct while another doesn't seem to care about accuracy?

- Why does a child succeed with one teacher and fail with another?

Working with the diversities within us should also enable us to deal with the diversities of preferences within and among our students. There are, therefore, dualities and their respective choices between us and our students. It is not enough then simply to be aware of our own preferences. We must, simultaneously, be aware of the preferences of our students. These diversities are represented as issues of:

- personality types
- learning styles
- teaching styles
- curriculum content, and
- assessment techniques

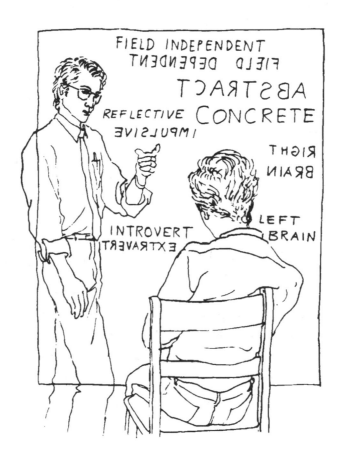

Working With Diversity: Messages to Be Read

Each student behavior or learning style presents itself as a message to be read. A traditional approach to understanding or describing our students has been to collect information about what the students knew rather than how they learned. We would ask questions such as;

- What are his reading and math levels?
- What skills has he demonstrated?
- What content has he mastered?
- What are his intellectual capacities?
- What are his work habits?

A problem with this type of assessment is that we find only a part of the information we need. It is as if we were working on understanding a role with only half a script. Defining a learner in terms of what s/he knows, rather than who s/he is and how s/he functions, results in characterizations that lead to stereotyping and pigeonholing, e.g., that the student is smart, dull, fast, slow, an independent worker, or one needing continual assistance. Such generalizations do little to help us understand or communicate more effectively with our students. If we are to reach and teach more students more effectively, we must learn to read and respond to the messages of student diversity.

In short, we must become as aware of how our students' diversities affect their learning as we are aware of what they learn. We must also become as aware of how our preferences affect our teaching as we are aware of what we teach. Dealing with diversity may then be interpreted as a communications challenge between teacher and learner. To read and respond constructively to our students' and our own preferences is the job of teaching.

Working With Diversity:
Teaching as Decision-Making

In order to read our students' messages and to resolve the duality of content versus process we must look at a great deal more than just the relationships of the student to some required content. Rather, we must look at the interaction among the teacher, the student, and the content to be learned. In this interaction or triangle of relationships, the role of the teacher is that of decision-maker. Mosston states that "All conscious teaching behavior is a chain of decision-making."[2] Decisions must be made continually about what students need to know, how students learn, and how we ourselves can teach more effectively. In order to become effective decision-makers we will need to understand our own behavior, the behavior of our students, and the nature of the curriculum or content to be taught. Decision-making

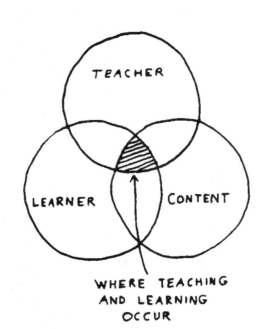

WHERE TEACHING
AND LEARNING
OCCUR

employing the triangle of relationships can be analyzed in three parts: first, decisions about the teaching act itself (e.g., teaching style, instructional strategies, class climate, physical setting, evaluation procedures, etc.); second, decisions about the learner (e.g., learning styles and profiles; physical, emotional, social, and intellectual needs, etc.); and third, decisions about the curriculum (e.g., content, quality, performance level, order and sequence, materials, mode and media, etc.). In short, the teacher is a decision-maker looking at multiple variables on each dimension of the triangle, as well as the three dimensions in relation to one another. Furthermore, the decision-making process occurs within an environment (e.g., a community, a school, a class and sets of relationships). Thus the issues of how and what are always place-specific and time-specific. Because teaching and learning involves teacher-student relationships, the process is always dynamic. The relationships may be pictured as follows:

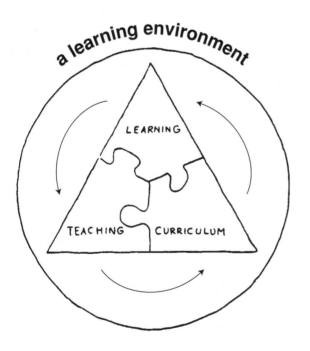

Working With Diversity: Improved Decision-Making Through Self-Understanding

If we, as teachers, are to achieve the goal of improved decision-making, a logical place to begin is with a well-focused self-analysis. We need to become sensitive to our own preferences for the ways in which we teach and learn, and to indicate how these preferences may affect our attitudes and behaviors regarding curriculum and learner needs.

In the teacher-student relationship, we, as the classroom authority figures, can project our attitudes onto our pupils with positive or detrimental effects. Understanding the factors affecting our preferences enables us to look more objectively at our students. Identifying personal preferences in ourselves will help us see our students as the unique individuals they are. The recognition of preferences will help us interpret and evaluate their work according to their own strengths.

Understanding the impact of our preferences is particularly important in the relationship between teacher and students because of the power inherent in the teacher's role. No matter how much we try to distribute that power, there is no way to deny the role we play in "approving" learning styles. That approval or validation power has life-shaping or life-retarding potential. The teacher has the ultimate authority to evaluate the student's performance. She provides feedback, not only in the form of grades, but also by the more subtle and unintentional messages internalized by the student as "you're good," or "you're no good." Whether we are aware of it or not, we send messages to students about their worth, and these messages reflect our own personal attitudes, beliefs, feelings, and ego needs.

Working With Diversity:
The Need for Validation

All of us, teachers as well as students, need to be validated if we are to learn and work more effectively. Each of us must feel that our own personal style of learning and working has worth and is valued. Our classrooms should be the places where we experiment with what best validates the students' unique qualities. School should not be a "win—lose," but rather a "win—win" environment. Each individual learner and teacher should feel that what he brings to the teaching relationship is meaningful and has value. Students and teachers who are validated not only feel better about themselves, but are less threatened by others. They are more often willing to take risks, to try new things, and to learn from their mistakes.

When we as teachers achieve greater personal awareness and understand better the factors influencing our preferences, we can begin to identify those same factors in our students. Such self-validation will lend itself to increased acceptance, appreciation, and understanding of the students committed to our care.

2

CHAPTER TWO

Overview Of The Thoughtful Education Model

Introduction

The Thoughtful Education Model was designed to assist teachers in dealing successfully with the diversity they confront in their classrooms. The model is based upon the seminal thinking and pioneering research of the Swiss psychiatrist Carl Gustav Jung. The model is a flexible and creative, yet organized approach for teachers to employ in classroom decision-making. The model provides a framework for improving the decision-making process across the three basic dimensions of the teaching/learning act, i.e.:

- the ability to analyze, categorize and develop curriculum according to pertinent cognitive and affective processes
- the ability to determine a student's dominant learning style and profile
- the ability to select and implement teaching strategies appropriate to the student's needs and the curriculum to be learned

Why Thoughtful Education?

We searched for years to find a name for our comprehensive model. We needed a name that emphasized the wholeness of the model as well as the recognition of both the cognitive and affective demands of learning.

Look at the word "thought." What comes to mind are the processes of analysis, inference, comparative capacity, evidence and reasonableness, i.e., the processes of cognition or knowing. When one adds the suffix "ful" then the word's meaning is expanded to include the concepts of caring, sharing, considerateness, empathy and personal involvement, i.e., the processes of affect or feeling. Hence to be a thoughtful educator means to be aware of both the cognitive and feeling dimensions of all learning tasks. And, like the polar-based model from which it comes, the dynamic tension between cognition/thinking and affect/feeling conveys the balance that must be maintained for effective teaching and learning to occur. In short, working with diversity means the teacher plans for and implements both dimensions in all her instruction.

Jung's Theory of Personality Type and Implications for Education[1]

The specific research underlying the Thoughtful Education Model comes from Jung's work on psychological types first published in 1921. Jung, the father of Analytical Psychology, was a major architect of psychoanalytic theory, and colleague of Sigmund Freud and Alfred Adler. Jung's theory identified four behavioral functions that, in various combinations, constitute personality type: sensing, intuition, thinking, and feeling. He also identified two attitudes toward life: introversion and extroversion.

Jung's theories of personality emerged from his observations on how people collected information, and how they made judgments about that same information in terms of its personal significance. A central theme in Jung's theory is that much apparently random variety in human behavior is due to the dependencies individuals develop for certain functions over their opposites.

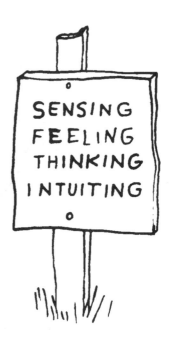

Jung came to his early observations concerning perception and judgment with the following reflections:

"I had always been impressed by the fact that there are a surprising number of people who never use their minds . . .

I was also surprised to find many intelligent and wide-awake people who lived (as far as one could make out) as if they had never learned to use their sense organs. They did not see the things before their eyes, hear the words sounding in their ears, or notice the things they touched or tasted. Some lived without being aware of the state of their own bodies.

There were others who seemed to live in a most curious condition of consciousness, as if the state they had arrived at today were final, with no possibility of change, or as if the world and the psyche were static and would remain so forever. They seemed devoid of all imagination, and they entirely and exclusively depended upon their sense-perceptions. Chances and possibilities did not exist in their world; future was just the repetition of the past.

I am trying here to give the reader a glimpse of my own first impressions when I began to observe the many people I met. It soon became clear to me, however, that the people who used their minds were those who thought—that is, who applied their intellectual faculty in trying to adapt themselves to people and circumstances. And the equally intelligent people who did not think were those who sought and found their way by feeling.

These four functional types correspond to the obvious means by which consciousness obtains its orientation to experience. **Sensation** (i.e., sense perception) tells you that something exists. **Thinking** tells you what it is; **Feeling** tells you whether it is agreeable or not; and **Intuition** tells you from whence it comes and where it is going."[2]

Jung pictured the opposing functions in the form of a mandala, i.e., each function representing a universal characteristic. The simple model is as follows:

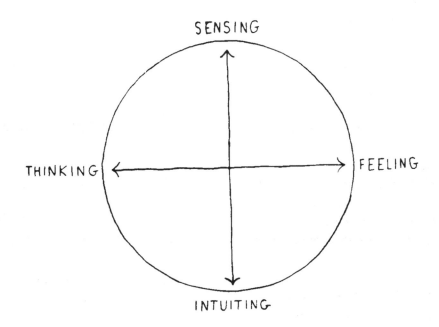

These four functions are explained in detail in Chapter Five.

PSYCHOLOGICAL TYPES*

	ST	SF	NF	NT
People who prefer:	SENSING + THINKING	SENSING + FEELING	INTUITION + FEELING	INTUITION + THINKING
focus their attention on:	Facts	Facts	Possibilities	Possibilities
and handle these with:	Impersonal analysis	Personal warmth	Personal warmth	Impersonal analysis
Thus they tend to become:	Practical and matter-of-fact	Sympathetic and friendly	Enthusiastic & insightful	Logical and ingenious
and find scope for their abilities in:	Technical skills with facts and objects	Practical help and services for people	Understanding & communicating with people	Theoretical & technical developments
for example:	Applied science Business Production Construction Etc.	Patient care Community service Teaching Sales Etc.	Behavioral science Literature & art Research Teaching Etc.	Physical science Research Management Forecasts & analysis Etc.

*Copyright, Isabel Briggs Myers, 1976. Used with the Permission of the Center for Application of Psychological Types, Gainesville, Fla.

Many authors have interpreted and applied Jung's framework for analyzing behaviors. Some authors have treated the functions in isolation from one another, whereas others, at Jung's suggestion, have paired the functions for a more comprehensive view of behavior. For example, Isabel Briggs Myers, the developer of the Myers Briggs Type Indicator[3], an instrument used to assess psychological type, has paired the perception and judgment functions.

Jung's theories of type and their practical applications were brought to the attention of educators through the efforts of Isabel Briggs Myers and the Center for Application of Psychological Type in Gainesville, Florida. The center's extensive work and research using the Myers Briggs Type Indicator provided educators with a practical tool for examining personality type and its implications for analyzing teaching and learning behaviors. The Thoughtful Education Model, by adopting and pairing the behaviors common to each function, provides the teacher with a common set of behavioral terms that apply equally to decisions affecting teaching, the diagnosis of learning styles, and the development and/or classification of curriculum objectives.

The chart which follows identifies teaching and learning behaviors by styles using the paired Jungian functions. The chart provides the teacher with a ready reference for making matches, for utilizing learning styles in curriculum planning, and for the selection of teaching strategies.

TEACHING AND LEARNING BEHAVIORS BY STYLES

SF	ST	NT	NF

TEACHERS MAY BE CHARACTERIZED AS:

SF	ST	NT	NF
• Nurturers	• Trainers	• Intellectual Challengers	• Facilitators
• Supporters	• Information Givers	• Inquirers	• Stimulators
• Empathizers	• Instructional Managers	• Theoreticians	• Creators/Originators

LEARNERS MAY BE CHARACTERIZED AS:

SF	ST	NT	NF
• Sympathetic	• Realistic	• Logical	• Curious
• Friendly	• Practical	• Intellectual	• Insightful
• Interpersonally Oriented	• Matter of Fact	• Knowledge Oriented	• Imaginative

CURRICULUM OBJECTIVES EMPHASIZE:

SF	ST	NT	NF
• Positive Self	• Basic Skills	• Critical Thinking	• Creative Thinking
• Socialization	• Acquisition of Concept	• Concept Development	• Moral Development

LEARNING ENVIRONMENTS EMPHASIZE:

SF	ST	NT	NF
• Personal warmth	• Purposeful Work	• Discovery	• Originality
• Interaction and Collaboration	• Organization and Competition	• Inquiry and Independence	• Flexibility and Imagination

INSTRUCTIONAL STRATEGIES EMPHASIZE:

SF	ST	NT	NF
• Personal and Social Awareness	• Behavior Modification	• Information Processing	• Self-Expression
• Group Projects	• Practice and Drill	• Research	• Imagination
• Personal Sharing	• Convergent Thinking Tasks	• Inductive Reasoning	• Divergent Thinking
• Oral Reports	• Demonstrations	• Written Reports	• Creative-Artistic Expression
• Communications	• Producing Products	• Problem-Solving	• Values Clarification

TEACHING STRATEGIES INCLUDE:

SF	ST	NT	NF
• Group Investigations	• Programmed Instruction	• Inquiry Training	• Inductive Learning
• Pair-Share	• Command Style Teaching	• Concept Attainment	• Synectics
• Classroom Meetings	• Mastery Learning	• Concept Formation	• Information Search
• Reciprocal Learning	• Team Games, Tournaments	• Reading for Meaning	• Boundary-breaking (breaking mind sets)
• Peer Tutoring	• Drill and Repetition	• Use of Socratic Methods of Questioning	• Analyzing and Working with Moral Dilemmas
• Sequencing Faces	• Graduated Difficulty	• Problem-solving	• Creative Problem Solving
• Lab Training	• Circles Within Circles	• Main Idea	
• Semrad's Steps	• Memorization	• Tangrams	
• Pre-Modeling		• Comprehensive Planning	
• Team Games, Tournaments			

ASSESSMENT PROCEDURES INCLUDE:

SF	ST	NT	NF
• Personal Journals	• Objective Tests	• Open-Ended Questions	• Fluency of Expression
• Sociograms	• Checklists	• Essays	• Flexibility of Response
• Oral Reports	• Behavioral Objectives	• Demonstration of Abilities to Apply, Synthesize, Interpret, Integrate, Analyze, Evaluate	• Originality of Response
• Ranking Procedures	• Use of Mechanical Devices		• Elaboration of Detail
• Trained Observations	• Demonstrations of Specific Skills	• Think Divergently	• Development of Aesthetic Criteria
• Collection of Unobtrusive Data	• Criterion Referenced Tests		• Producing Creative Products
• Self-Reporting			• Observations of Value Systems in Action
			• Unobtrusive Data Collection

The Best Possible Matches

Improving the quality of the teaching-learning relationship depends, first of all, on the teacher's ability to make the best possible "match" between the student's learning preferences, the curriculum to be taught, and the teaching style to be used.

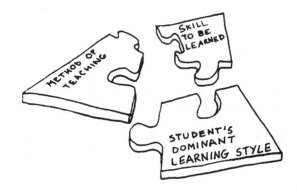

Making matches requires a thorough knowledge of instructional choices, e.g., teaching strategies, activities, materials, and classroom environment. Making matches also requires clear goals for student (and teacher) attainment.

Jung spoke of two major objectives for psychic development that have clear parallels for teaching, learning and the matching process. He called these two opposing objectives "perfection" and "completion."

By perfection Jung meant the need to develop our own particular strengths or abilities to the maximum. The opposite choice is to strive after completion. This striving attempts to develop strengths across all of our actual as well as potential abilities. Perfection (never really possible) occurs in one's dominant style. Completion occurs in one's profile over the lesser developed functions.

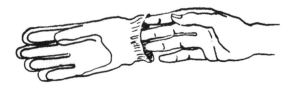

Basically there are two types of matches. First, the matching of student learning style, content mastery, and teaching techniques based on the goal of perfection. This type of match emphasizes "congruity." Congruence occurs when the student is consistently provided with opportunities to learn in his own most preferred or dominant style. Such matches tend to provide approval and success experiences for students.

A second matching process is based on the goal of completion. This type of matching emphasizes fluency and flexibility. Fluency occurs when the student is consistently provided with opportunities to learn in different styles through the development of different competencies. Fluency and flexibility matches lead to the student's appreciation of his or her ability to operate in different learning styles.

In making these matches the teacher exercises power to approve or validate the pupil, to enhance his self-concept, and to increase his repertoire of cognitive and affective skills. Where the teacher's goal is perfection, the objective of making matches is congruence. Where the teacher's goal is completion, the objectives are both congruence and fluency-flexibility.

3

CHAPTER THREE

Stepping Into The Process Of Self-Assessment

Introduction

Jung recognized very early in the development of psychoanalytical models the need for practitioners to undergo therapy. Such analysis was, and remains, a critical component of the training process for psychoanalysts.

It is no less true for those of us working in the other helping professions. Self-analysis is necessary if we are to become aware of our own preferential behaviors, and to avoid imposing our beliefs and idiosyncrasies on those with whom we work. Likewise, those of us who assist others in learning must first become aware of our own learning preferences, not only to teach more effectively, but also to be more open to the learning preferences and values of others.

Our common sense reminds us that, as teachers, we tend to teach as we like to be taught, and we focus our efforts on those issues or topics that we find most significant or valuable.

The effects of these experiences and values on our teaching behaviors are often unknown to us. This manual will assist you in uncovering the teaching decisions we make from unexamined impulse. We will seek to answer these questions: Why do we behave as we do? And what do we really know about ourselves as learners and as teachers?

Self-knowledge is the first step toward change. Thinkers down through the ages have long recognized that self-knowledge leads to greater creativity, a less distorted perception of reality and greater freedom.

Karen Horney, a world famous analyst, reinforces this connection between self-knowledge and freedom by maintaining that growing self-knowledge renders "…a person free from inner bondages," and thus "…makes him free for the development of more of his potentialities."[1]

Frank Goble, writing about Abraham Maslow's Needs Hierarchy, comments as follows:

"When a person understands himself he will understand his basic needs and true motivation and will learn to behave in a manner which will satisfy those needs. Self-understanding will also enable one to understand and relate to other people more effectively."[2]

This manual on teacher self-assessment will guide you through a series of self-insight experiences. Your openness to these experiences and your willingness to apply its resulting insights will be reflected in your teaching effectiveness.

Some Basic Ideas to Consider

As with the runner preparing for a race, some warm-up time is essential before stepping into the "Who am I?" task. As a warm-up we first recommend that you find yourself a quiet comfortable spot. In this setting explore your own thoughts and feelings and focus on how you feel, contrary to how you think you should feel. In effect you are being challenged to trust yourself enough to be you, and to search for your own "center" of being. There are, after all, no right or wrong answers. There is only you, your feelings about yourself, and your perceptions of yourself. In short, the degree to which you trust yourself to be open and honest is the degree to which these exercises will be profitable.

In this introspective warm-up period, the two major hurdles are the decisions to commit yourself to being honest and to accept the insights identified even if they are uncomfortable or confusing. Above all, search for the responses from within yourself rather than from the expectations of others. The question is not whether it is all right to be what you are; whether you feel good about yourself or not. You simply are! Even the intense personal recognition that you wish to be something else is a statement of what you are now.

The warm-up period also includes the need to reflect on yourself in terms of the past, the present, and your hopes for the future. This boils down to asking yourself questions such as:

- What do I like, dislike, admire or regret about my past?
- Who am I, and how do I feel now?
- What behaviors would I like to change?

Robert Heinlein may have said it best: "We have the dead past, the dying moment, and the ever-living always-emerging future. The future is all that we can change."

Finally, there is a little Walter Mitty in all of us. Our peripheral and fleeting ambitions, those dreams that awaken us in the night or are remembered in the morning, may suggest some directions for future explorations.

A second major point for consideration is the need to solicit information about yourself from others. This may be done in pairs or in small groups. It may be a sharing session, or the invitation to honest criticism.

Human feedback enables us to see ourselves more as others see us. Obtaining specific, descriptive, non-judgmental feedback regarding our behavior from those with whom we live and work (e.g., students, peers, spouses and significant others) is an indispensable source of information for self-analysis and self-growth. Such sharing can result in the recognition that we all have basic strengths and weaknesses in common. Trust in the responses of others is, in itself, a valuable insight into selfhood. Joe Luft and Harry Ingram developed a simple system for categorizing information about the self.[3] These same categories may be useful to you in working through these exercises.

Knowledge can be grouped as a) knowledge about myself that I know and that others know; b) knowledge about myself that I know and others do not know; c) knowledge about myself that others know that I don't know; and d) knowledge that is unknown both to myself and to others (i.e., our preconscious and unconscious states).

A third point for consideration is that self-knowledge is a never-ending process. Self-insights may come slowly. There is a need, therefore, to work consciously for self-insight. We can create a more receptive mind by immersing ourselves in the self-discovery process. The exercises may be repeated at intervals for assimilation and new growth.

Things about myself that I:

KNOW   DON'T KNOW

Things about myself that the other:

KNOWS

DOES NOT KNOW

A fourth point is that the process of self-discovery itself, the questioning and searching, is as important as the answers. How we come to grips with the personal content of each exercise and instrument is critical to interpreting the significance of the findings. Becoming is the essence of being. In short, the actions we take as a result of thinking and feeling our way through these exercises are the payoffs!

We are talking about personal growth as change. Growth, as a process, suggests the continuing need to ask yourself the same questions repeatedly. Today's conclusions will be tomorrow's questions.

A fifth and final consideration involves not only the personal working and reworking of the questions and exercises, but also the sharing of the exercises with your students. You, as the teacher-facilitator, can, in the process of presenting parallel activities to your pupils, learn more about yourself. In fact, the exercises themselves may become a curriculum for self-knowledge and self-identity.

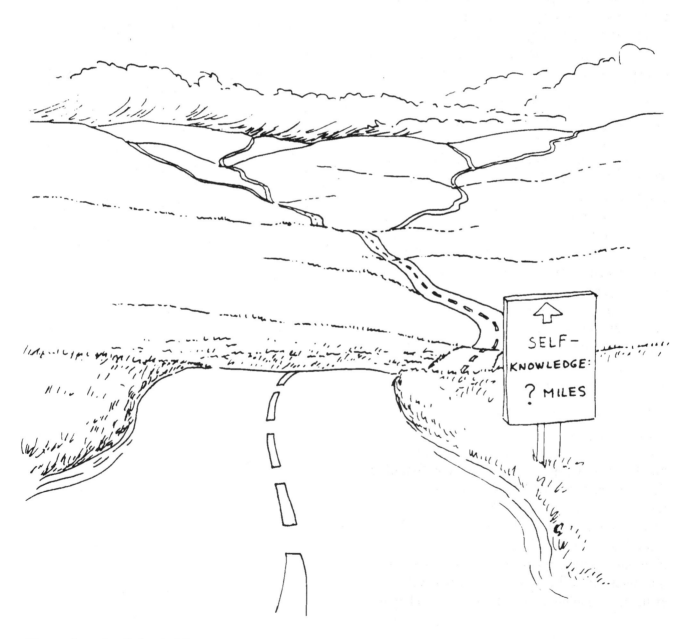

A Variety of Approaches

No one way of collecting information about ourselves will provide a complete and accurate picture. At best we can only capture a shadow or reflection of "what is." This is why we need to use a combination of instruments, procedures and techniques to help us answer the central question, "Who am I?"

A number of approaches will be used, therefore, to help you work through the processes of self-assessment. The activities are grouped in three clusters.

The first set of activities includes steps for looking at your behaviors across each of the three dimensions of personality functioning identified by Jung (e.g., preferences for sensing or intuiting, feeling or thinking, and introversion or extroversion).

The second set of activities is designed to stimulate your thinking about yourself as a learner and about how your preferences affect your attitude and behavior in your classroom. The chapter includes a number of open-ended warm-up activities to introduce you to the self-assessment process and to focus your thinking on your preferred learning behaviors. Furthermore, you will be asked to take the **Learning Style Inventory**, a 125-item diagnostic self-projection test based on Jung's theories of type as modified by the authors for the identification of learning styles. Also included are descriptions of the four basic learning styles and procedures for analyzing and scoring the **Learning Style Inventory**.

In the third set of activities an additional focusing step is taken as you look specifically at your behaviors as a teacher. Included are a number of warm-up activities and the **Teaching Style Inventory**, a diagnostic self-projection test for looking at teaching behavior across ten variables: classroom atmosphere, teaching techniques, planning, preferred qualities of children, teacher/student interaction, classroom management, discipline, teaching behavior, evaluation, and educational goals. This chapter also includes descriptions of the four basic teaching styles and procedures for analyzing and scoring the **Teaching Style Inventory**.

Before you begin the activities in the following chapter, we suggest you make some decisions about the following:

- How will you handle your record-keeping functions? Will you keep a log or diary? Will you write directly in the manual? Will you need a tape recorder?

- How will you process this information? Will you work by yourself? Will you work with a friend: a small group? A large group? How will you identify these people?

- Are you in a setting which is comfortable enough for you to explore your thoughts and feelings?

After these initial decisions have been made, it is time to begin. Self-knowledge, to paraphrase William Shakespeare, has an appetite that grows by what it feeds on. The more we learn about ourselves and others, the more we want to learn. The old adage that the unexamined life is not worth living has a far more frightening counterpart, or as Shakespeare said, "There are no prisons so confining as those of which we are unaware." If as adults and teachers we expect our students to grow, we can do no less ourselves.

Good luck, and enjoy yourself.

4

CHAPTER FOUR

Self-Discovery Using Jung's Definitions Of Type

Who Am I?

In the pages which follow you will be repeatedly asked the question "who am I?" in terms of these basic Jungian constructs.

The Perception Functions

The two ways, Jung said, of perceiving or finding out about persons, places or things, are through our senses, or, on the opposite pole of this same axis, through our intuition. Sensing (S) is the gathering of facts about a situation. When we use the sensing function, we become aware of things as they appear. The sensor assumes that what he sees is what exists. Sensing deals with the shape, color, texture, and arrangement of things. Sensing describes for us the actual state of things.

Jung's Definitions of Type

Jung articulated a critical concept for interpreting behavior by stipulating that all behaviors are the result of two opposite yet interdependent functions, i.e., two functions for perceiving (sensing and intuition), and two functions for judging (feeling and thinking).

Jung also identified an attitudinal orientation modifying the perception and judgment functions. These attitudes he termed introversion and extroversion. These attitudes are reflected in a person's preferred way of processing ideas and tasks.

Intuition (N),* the opposite pole on the perception axis, is the ability to perceive the inner meaning and relationships of what is occurring, i.e., to see possibilities for what might be or to make interpretations. The intuitor, unlike the sensor, does not always believe that what he sees is what exists, but rather looks to what the potential significance of the situation might be. Where the sensor sees and then believes, the intuitor believes and then sees.

Everyone uses both sensing and intuition but not at precisely the same time, and not, in most cases, with equal liking or facility. Preferences develop like muscles. The more they are used, the stronger they become. Preferences for perception, then, are the comfortable behaviors that we each develop over time. Perception functions, unlike judgment functions, however, are nonrational, i.e., they tend not to be consciously motivated processes.

*The N is used for intuition to distinguish it from the I of introversion.

SENSING VERSUS INTUITING

THE PERCEPTION OPPOSITES

(How the data are acquired)

From: Seeing
　　　　Hearing
　　　　Touching
　　　　Tasting
　　　　Smelling

(How the data are acquired)

From: Genetic signals
　　　　One's personal unconscious
　　　　One's nervous structure
　　　　Hereditary factors
　　　　One's collective unconscious
　　　　Archetypal energies

PRACTICAL POSSIBLE

(Forms for perception include)

Color
Shape
Form
"What is?" Concreteness
Tangibility
Linearity, sequence
Digital, one by one, messages
Manipulation

(Forms for perception include)

Patterns
Meanings
Possibilities
Symbol Systems
Configurations
Abstractions
Analogic (seeing things whole)
"What might be?"

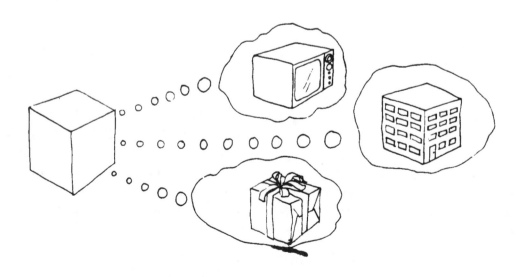

The behaviors below are characteristic of the two types of perception functions. They are juxtaposed for ease of comparison.

THE PERCEPTION OPPOSITES

VERSUS

SENSING	**INTUITING**
interested in facts	interested in ideas
focuses attention on the here and now, what is	focuses attention on the future and what could be
interested in doing things which have immediate practical use	interested in possibilities beyond what is present, obvious or known
prefers to take action on ideas rather than talking about them	prefers to generate ideas rather than be responsible for putting them into action
comfortable with a standard way of doing things	comfortable doing things their own way
impatient when details become complicated	patient with complicated situations
trusts hard work and perspiration	trusts inspirations, visions and imagination
prefers verbal directness	prefers elaboration, metaphoric expression and poetry
tries to complete work as quickly as possible	works continuously when interested in what they are doing
wants to achieve immediate tangible results	wants to achieve important new solutions to long-range problems
enjoys using skills already learned more than learning new ones	enjoys learning new skills more than using them
works more steadily with realistic ideas of how long it will take	works with bursts of energy, powered by enthusiasm with slack periods in between

Make a mark on the continuum that best
describes your perception preference.

Strongly prefer
immediate, real, practical
facts of experience

Strongly prefer
looking for possibilities,
meanings and relationships

Reading through these two opposing sets
of behaviors may have been confusing because
you may have recognized yourself on both sides
of the column. Since we all operate to greater
or lessor degrees in all the functions, it is
understandable that you would identify familiar
behaviors from both columns. For most of us,
however, one group of behaviors is more
characteristic than the other, i.e., we have a
greater preference for one function than for
its opposite.

The sensing-intuition preferences vary from
extremely sensing dominant to extremely
intuiting dominant, and all the shades of
position in between. Where on the perception
continuum above does your preference lie?
Do you rely more on your senses or on your
intuition to understand what is happening
around you? Place a mark on the rope (but not
in the exact center) which best represents how
you understand your perception preference.
Remember, Jung cites these preferences as
opposites, i.e., our preferences fall either toward
sensing, or toward intuition, but not to both
equally, and not simultaneously.

The Judgment Function

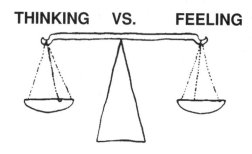

Next, Jung said there were two basic and
opposite ways for analyzing how we make
judgments about the data or information perceived.
The judgment processes are thinking and feeling.

The thinking function tends to predict the
logical result of any actions we may take.
Thinking persons tend to decide impersonally
and to think in terms of cause and effect.
The thinker searches for facts, logical truths,
verifiable information from authoritative
sources, and well-defined procedures for
solving problems. The thinker decides, based
on external and verifiable information, what
is true and what is false.

The opposite judgment function is that of feeling. Feeling judgments are made on the basis of the personal import of any stimulus, rather than on logic, external evidence or cause and effect.

These judgment functions, unlike the perception functions, are rational in that they are conscious self-initiated mental processes.

Jung's theory says that we tend to rely on one judgment function over its opposite. While everyone uses both judgment functions, the feeler searches for what he likes and that with which he feels comfortable. The thinker, for example, becomes skillful in dealing with those phenomena that behave in an orderly, rational, and logical manner. The thinker's emphases are objective and impersonal analysis based on the demonstrability of the evidence.

The thinker makes decisions by weighing the facts; including the unpleasant ones. The feeler, on the other hand, tends to be more skillful in dealing with people, is more sympathetic, empathetic, appreciative, tactful and friendly. When making decisions, the feeler gives emphasis to personal values, including the feelings of others. The thinker lets his head guide his heart; ideas generate feelings and not the reverse. For the feeler the intellect is guided by emotions; the heart rules the head.

... like or dislike ...

FEELING

... true or false ...

THINKING

Thinking VERSUS Feeling

THE JUDGMENT OPPOSITES

VERSUS

THINKING
(How perceptions are judged)

- by logic
- by citing external evidence
- by asking "is it true or false?"
- by being objective through cognition or intellect
- by looking for facts and reasons

FEELING
(How perceptions are judged)

- by asking "do I like it or not?"
- using one's own internal evidence
- by asking "Is it good or bad?"
- by trusting feelings
- by looking to one's past experience and what one values

The behaviors below are characteristic of the two types of judgment functions. They are juxtaposed for ease of comparison and contrast.

THE JUDGMENT OPPOSITES

VERSUS

THINKING	FEELING
makes decisions impersonally based on logical analysis	makes decisions based on personal feelings
responds to logic, reason and truth	responds to his own and other people's likes and dislikes
likes to figure things out before taking action	tends to be spontaneous: may be "way up" or "way down"
exhibits consistent and predictable behavior	work is scattered, sometimes messy and unorganized
interested in detailed factual information (charts, graphs, maps)	interested in things that have personal meaning
tends to be independent of other people for approval	seeks the approval of other people
needs to be treated fairly	needs praise
may seem hard-hearted	enjoys pleasing people
enjoys arguing a point	enjoys harmony and agreement
relies on organizational skills	relies on relational skills
tends to be objective	tends to be sympathetic

The thinking-feeling dependencies vary from extremely thinking dominant to extremely feeling dominant and include all the shades in between. Look again at the behaviors below. Where on the thinking-feeling continuum do you place yourself? Do you rely more on externally verified determinations of truth or on personal likes and dislikes? Place an X on the rope below indicating your self-perception relative to thinking or feeling. Remember your self-assessment position must be on one side of the axis or the other. It cannot be in the center.

Place a mark at the point on the continuum which you think best describes your judgmental preference.

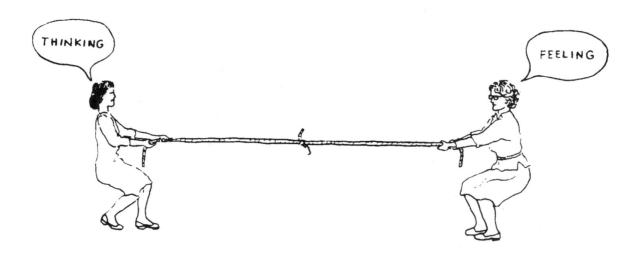

Strongly prefer
considers data objectively,
impersonally, and questions
where decisions may lead

Strongly prefer
considers data subjectively
in terms of likes
and comfort level, and
is very aware of the
feelings of others

Introversion and Extroversion

Jung identified a third dimension which describes how one processes ideas after having collected the data. This bi-polar dimension he termed introversion/extroversion. These two concepts are critical to an understanding of Jung's thinking. Thus, in addition to an individual's dependencies for certain paired functions, there is also a fundamental orientation or attitude toward life and learning. This attitude, i.e., introversion or extroversion, determines how the individual operates ("thinks" in a generic sense), regardless of his perception and judgment preferences.

The extrovert is characterized as one who focuses his psychic energies on the external world of events and objects. He is influenced primarily by his surroundings. His interests have an outward movement toward people and external phenomena.

The introvert, on the opposite pole, directs his mental energies inward toward issues of subjective interest. He is influenced by his own intentions, rather than by external events. His interests tend to focus on the subjects that can best be dealt with internally, reflectively, contemplatively, and in detail.

The following attitudes are characteristics of the introverted and extroverted in work or learning situations.

THE ATTITUDINAL OPPOSITES

VERSUS

INTROVERSION	EXTROVERSION
• likes quiet for concentration	• likes variety and action
• likes to work alone	• likes to work with others
• tends not to be talkative	• talks a great deal
• generally reluctant initially to share feelings and information	• open; eager to share feelings and information
• tends to be hard to get to know	• easy to know
• thinks, contemplates extensively before taking action	• acts/reacts quickly to new situations or new challenges
• tends not to mind working on one project for long periods of time	• tends to be impatient with long-term tasks
• dislikes interruptions	• doesn't seem to mind interruptions
• likes to perform for himself	• likes to perform for others
• careful with details	• tends to dislike complicated procedures
• prefers to listen	• prefers the interaction that comes in talking with others

Because the extrovert operates "in the open," involved as he is with the world outside himself, he tends to be more easily understood, more outgoing, more at ease in groups, and more willing to be channeled in terms of new interests and activities. He tends to be more verbal and socially aggressive.

The introvert, on the opposite pole, directs his mental energies inward toward issues of subjective interest. He is influenced more by his own intentions than by external events. The introvert is more involved with the meanings of his own internal images and values and may appear more demanding than the extrovert.

As a result, he tends not to be a joiner, not to be easily led, difficult to read, and in a world of his own.

Place a mark at that point on the continuum which you think best describes your attitudinal preference.

These two attitudes are mutually exclusive. While they cannot peacefully coexist they do alternate in emphasis depending on the circumstances of choice. Thus, one attitude tends to predominate such that attitude characterizes how the mind processes those data perceived and judged most of the time.

Place a mark at that point on the continuum which you think best describes your attitudinal preference.

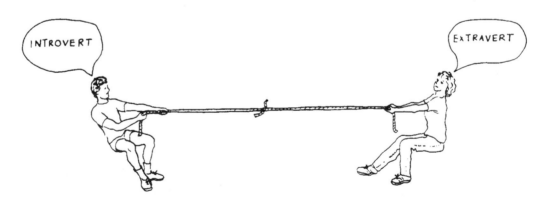

Strongly prefer
likes quiet for concentration
is careful about details
dislikes broad generalities

Strongly prefer
likes variety and action;
tends to work quickly;
dislikes complicated details;
enjoys group functions

Personality Types

Personality types are the results of sets of exercised preferences. The three sets of choices in combination represent eight (8) different personality types (i.e., four types x two attitudes).

Circle the single choice from each of the three dimensions of type to subjectively assess your own personality type. Extroversion (E) or Introversion (I), Sensing (S) or Intuiting (N), Thinking (T) or Feeling (F)

Transfer the first letter of each choice into the spaces provided. These three choices represent your own perceptions about how you function using the Jungian framework for understanding personality types.

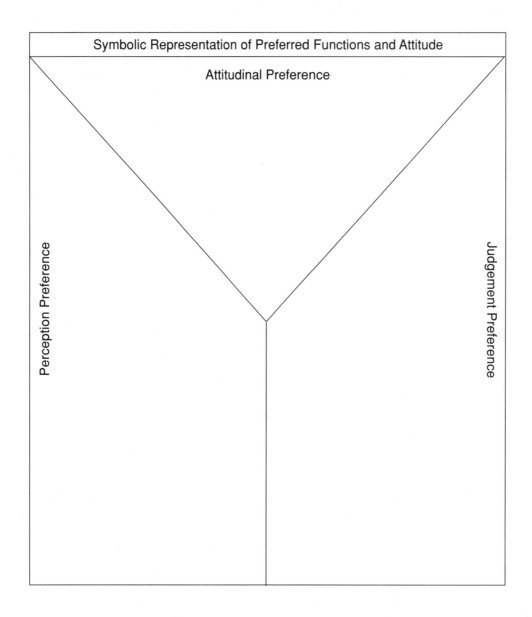

Symbolic Representation of Preferred Functions and Attitude

Attitudinal Preference

Perception Preference

Judgement Preference

To further clarify and reinforce your reasons for choosing your specific functions and attitude, briefly describe or interpret your three symbolic representations. Indicate the reasons for the choices you make.

Another way to express your preferences is to draw them symbolically. Using abstract symbols, stick figures, pictures or montages (and using colors), design pictures or images of yourself that express your three different preferences. Be as metaphoric or poetic as you wish. The point at issue is to let your mind identify those signs and symbols that best express for you your perception, judgment, and attitudinal preferences.

Description of symbolic representation and explanatory notes

Perception

_____

_____

_____

_____

_____

Judgement

_____

_____

_____

_____

_____

Attitude

_____

_____

_____

_____

_____

_____

_____

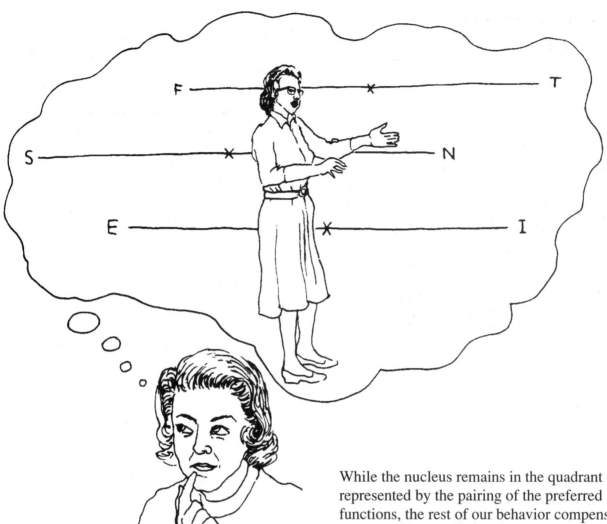

Now compare your subjective analysis of your type and your symbolic expressions with the behavioral descriptions which follow. These descriptions are characterizations of the eight personality types and are written in general terms to provide mental "pictures" of the types. The descriptions are stereotypic. No single person is exactly like any particular description.

As an aid or a mental picture for thinking about type, picture an amoeba. The amoeba has a nucleus and a jelly-like protoplasm that is constantly changing in size and shape. If the nucleus is compared to our dominant function or our natural preference, and the protoplasm represents the other less preferred functions, a picture of the complexity of type emerges.

While the nucleus remains in the quadrant represented by the pairing of the preferred functions, the rest of our behavior compensates in various proportions over the other behavioral pairings depending on the specific nature of the tasks involved. In other words, each of us operates in all four quadrants based on natural preference and the compensating behavior necessary to function in various roles and for various tasks. Therefore, no one person is any one style but is a combination of all four. The amoeba metaphor asks us to look beyond the immediately conscious notion of how we learn and function to the deeper understanding of how we experience life as perception, judgment, and attitudinal response.

As you read the descriptions, you may find that one type is an accurate description of your own personality with the exception of a few words or a phrase. If such is the case, we suggest that you focus on the overall appropriateness of the description as a self-indicator of your preference rather than on the points which may be atypical.

The Sensing-Feeling Personality Type (SF)

The Sensing-Feeling person perceives with his senses and makes decisions based on personal feelings of like or dislike rather than on impersonal logic. He focuses on facts primarily in terms of people.

Since the Sensing-Feeler prefers sensing to intuition, he tends to have a practical, "feet on the ground" attitude. He is a keen observer of human behavior and pays attention to the facts and details of his immediate surroundings. As a feeler he tends to be tactful, sympathetic, and interested in people. He acts on their behalf.

The Sensing-Feeling person is socially and emotionally aware. He is keenly aware of his own feelings and the feelings of others. He finds it difficult to take an analytical or detached point of view of things. He has excellent counseling abilities and often chooses to work in the helping professions. He is very involved in his own personal and emotional development, and he believes that without human relationships life has little meaning.

The **Extroverted Sensing-Feeler** is outgoing, talkative, and popular. He is fun to be with and enjoys having a good time. He is socially adept and good at working with others. He comes alive when interacting with people. He enjoys talking and likes to perform. He prefers jobs which deal with people and does his best thinking when talking to others. He finds it difficult to work alone or to express himself in a few words. He is usually optimistic and motivated by approval. He has a strong desire to belong and to be accepted. He is open with his feelings, gregarious, and good at working with others. He is a natural cooperator and committee person.

The **Introverted Sensing-Feeler**, like the extroverted Sensing-Feeler, has a keen interest in things that directly and visibly affect people's lives. Because of his introverted nature he prefers intense relationships with one or two special people rather than interacting with many different people. He is capable of deep and strong feelings but may not show them outwardly unless he feels comfortable enough to express himself. He may seem aloof or independent to those who do not know him. Those who are close to him realize that he is loyal, considerate, and deeply concerned about the feelings of others. He prefers to express his devotion and loyalty through deeds rather than words.

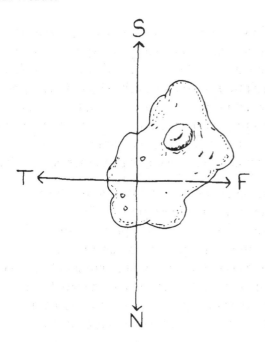

The Sensing-Thinking Personality Type (ST)

The Sensing-Thinking person perceives the world through his senses and thus lives in the "here and now." He relies on thinking to make decisions and is concerned more about logical consequences than personal feelings. The Sensing-Thinking personality perceives the world in terms of things tangible to the senses, rather than abstract ideas, theories, or models. He distrusts abstractions and therefore tends not to generalize. As a thinker he wants his ideas, plans, and decisions to be based on solid facts verified by logic. He holds facts to be the only basis for action.

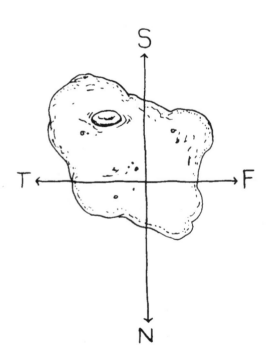

The Sensing-Thinker is self-sufficient. He desires emotional control and treats his own feelings objectively. He insists on control in himself and others. He is impatient with ambiguity and is comfortable with order and familiar surroundings. He prefers consistency to variation. He is decisive and seeks and needs early closure to queries or problems. He is respectful of rules and is comfortable following procedures. He is objective, practical, and expedient.

The **Extroverted Sensing-Thinker** is assertive, confident, and energetic. He is a good manager and enjoys getting things organized and done. He likes to take charge of a situation and give orders. He immediately recognizes what is necessary and works with speed and economy of effort to complete a task. He likes to work where he can achieve immediate visible and tangible results. He is action-oriented and finds it difficult not to act on a problem. He prefers to solve problems through trial and error by expertly applying and adapting past experiences. He enjoys physical and manual tasks and solving technical problems. He enjoys sports and is adept at physical activities. He has a "natural head" for business and organization.

The **Introverted Sensing-Thinker** is serious, disciplined, reserved, and thorough. He has a great capacity for facts and details. He considers planning a "must" and takes decision-making seriously. A sense of structure for himself and his environment is important. He enjoys quantifying information, measuring things, working with data, and listing facts. He is patient and accurate with details and skillful at organizing information.

The introverted Sensing-Thinker is self-sustaining and is unwilling to be in another's debt. As a worker he is able to apply himself for long periods of time. He is thorough and efficient and a great believer in economy of effort. He is willing to go through any amount of effort to complete a task if he sees the need for it, but dislikes doing things that don't make sense. He is good with his hands and enjoys individual sports and the outdoors. As an administrator, his practical judgment and memory for detail make him conservative and consistent.

The Intuitive-Thinking Personality Type (NT)

The Intuitive-Thinking person looks at the world through his intuition rather than his senses. Therefore, he is interested in abstract ideas, possibilities, and the meanings of things beyond the concrete or tangible. He relies on his thinking more than his feelings to make decisions. As a result, his thought processes tend to be logical, analytical, often critical, and generally impersonal. He is unlikely to be convinced by anything but reason.

The Intuitive-Thinker is theoretical, thinks more inductively, and generally is interested in the broad picture rather than specific details. He values facts mainly in relation to theory. He is knowledge-oriented, interested in intellectual pursuits, and is concerned about intellectual achievement.

The Intuitive-Thinker tends to conceptualize as a primary way of interpreting life. He is highly logical. He needs problems to solve. He is expert at finding new solutions and is often more interested in reaching solutions than in putting them into action. He takes pleasure in work which entails analysis or synthesis of logical components. He needs to know the reason for things and prefers to let his head guide his heart. His ideas generate his feelings. He is well informed and continually adds to his knowledge.

The **Extroverted Intuitive-Thinker** is intelligent, ingenious, and outspoken. He is highly verbal and has the capacity for leadership. He believes that words are power and may use them as weapons. He has a strong appetite for conversation and enjoys debating an issue and scoring points. He may argue either side of a question for the sake of intellectual satisfaction. He is resourceful at solving new and challenging problems and is good at anything that requires reasoning and intelligent discussion.

The extroverted Intuitive-Thinking person needs to be challenged intellectually. He dislikes routine and finds it difficult to apply himself to detail inapplicable to his interests. When projects become routine, he quickly loses interest. He prefers to turn to one new interest after another. He is most comfortable and effective in jobs which allow him to plan,

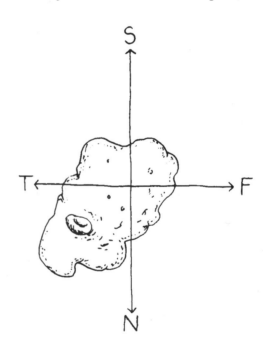

conceptualize, and organize with someone else being responsible for the details. He prefers to establish policy rather than to carry it out. He prefers long-range planning rather than detailed planning. He prefers to find solutions to problems rather than to carry out the solutions.

The extroverted Intuitive-Thinker desires power. He is competitive and needs to make an impact on what he is doing. He is unwilling to accept failure and may be overtly critical of himself and others. He is adept at leading people through the power of persuasion.

The **Introverted Intuitive-Thinker** is the most individualistic and most independent of all the types. He enjoys dealing with abstract theories and ideas and may be relatively indifferent to the material world. He prefers and needs to be alone to think, to research ideas, and to formulate theories. He has a strong sense of principle and may be somewhat detached or indifferent to the daily needs of the physical world. He has an intellectual toughness and may tend to ignore views and feelings of those who don't agree with him. He is self-critical and hard to comfort. He is determined, decisive, and often stubborn. He tends to drive himself in pursuit of an idea.

The introverted Intuitive-Thinker is good at scientific research, math, and other abstract or symbolic disciplines such as philosophy and psychology. He is quiet, reserved, and often respected for his "original mind." He is often skeptical. He may be logical to the point of hairsplitting. He has well-defined interests and needs to choose a career in which these interests can be pursued. He has exceptional ability to organize work and to carry it out.

The Intuitive-Feeling Personality Type (NF)

The Intuitive-Feeling person prefers to look at things with his intuition rather than his senses and hence is mainly interested in seeing possibilities beyond what is present, obvious, or known. Intuition heightens his understanding, long-range vision, insight, curiosity about new ideas, interest in the future, and tolerance for ambiguity. Since he prefers to make decisions with his feelings, his intuition is focused on

people, values, culture, and the arts. The Intuitive-Feeler is energetic, enthusiastic and imaginative. He views the world as undergoing constant change. In light of this perpetual motion he searches for new possibilities or new ways of doing things. He has an active imagination. He initiates original projects with impulsive bursts of energy for carrying them out. He often finds himself over committed because he has started more projects than he can complete. He begins projects with enthusiasm which may tend to dwindle as he moves closer to detail or completion. He is flexible. He fluctuates in mood from one extreme to the another. He has high tolerance for ambiguity and alternative belief systems. He is open to his own inspirations, motivations, and irrational impulses. He is creative and sensitive to beauty and to the aesthetic quality of things.

The Intuitive-Feeler is concerned about the future and problems of human welfare. He is idealistic, thinks in terms of values, and tries to clarify his beliefs. He is an innovator and serves as a catalyst for change. He often objects to things as they are and wants to bring about significant changes. He disregards status distinctions and prefers to pay attention to personal qualities. He believes that everyone is unique and is entitled to the same rights and considerations.

The **Extroverted Intuitive-Feeler** is a charismatic leader, high spirited, and responsive to the needs of others. He is skillful at motivating people. He generates enthusiasm and cooperation from others. He inspires others to act and to serve as catalysts for needed change. He tends to be irrepressible, talkative, and playful. He wants excitement and has high mood fluctuations.

The extroverted Intuitive-Feeler is able to improvise and is quick to formulate solutions to problems. He can do almost anything that he finds interesting and can find compelling reasons to justify what he does. He believes in his inspirations and will work tirelessly for some cause or activity that captures his imagination. His interests may make him unaware of things going on around him.

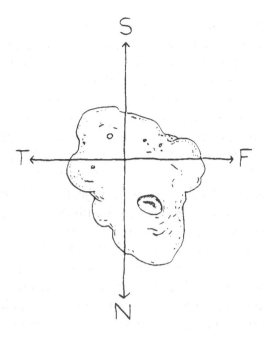

The extroverted Intuitive-Feeler is gifted at self-expression and may tend to use this gift in persuasion and explanation rather than in some written form. His interests in people and possibilities attract him to careers such as politics, psychology, teaching, counseling, and human relations.

The **Introverted Intuitive-Feeler** is idealistic, artistic, and empathetic. His is a complex personality with an active inner life of contemplation and spirituality. Outwardly he may appear cool and reserved but inwardly he has a great capacity for caring. He has a strong need to clarify his own beliefs. He needs to contribute toward the welfare of others. The introverted Intuitive-Feeler, more than any other type, demonstrates abilities to understand and appreciate psychic and spiritual forces. The introverted Intuitive-Feeler is often adept at reading and interpreting the emotions of others even before they may be aware of their feelings.

The introverted Intuitive-Feeler tends to be the most poetic of all types. He has an active imagination and views the world in terms of personal visions, images, possibilities, and premonitions of things to come. The introverted Intuitive-Feeler appreciates life's mysteries and is often seen by others as being mystical. He is able to imagine and construct profound and complex works of art. He is often adept at expressing

himself artistically both in speech and writing.

The introverted Intuitive-Feeler tends to be patient with complicated situations but impatient with routine detail. He reaches for success by being persistent and original. He is a quietly forceful but not a visible type of leader. He works well alone but also enjoys working with others. He tends to be respected by others because of the strength of his convictions and his clear principles.

Self-Reflection

If, after having studied the type characteristics you feel the preferences you selected form a good self-description, then these preferences probably represent a fair picture of your dominant attitude and style. If the description does not seem to fit, examine the other descriptions that have the same judgment or perception functions as your own. If the description still appears inappropriate the following explanations may be considered. First, perhaps one or more of the terms was unclear. Three of the four terms provide some special problems, e.g., **sensing** in English often has the connotation of a hunch, i.e., "I sense that something terrible is about to happen." (In Jung's usage this use of sense is the intuitive function). Sensing, for Jung, is restricted to what we know through our five senses.

Feeling as a term is confusing, too. Americans often use feeling as an emotive state, one of sentiment, rather than as a rational thought process of like or dislike.

Intuition is particularly difficult since we have no precise translation for its German equivalent. Intuition in this country is often confused with a special sense that operates mystically, e.g., a woman's intuition. In Jung's terms, intuition is the nonrational process by which the mind collects data in terms of its possibilities, patterns, and relationships. It is a pre-judgmental and synthesizing activity of non-consciously prompted origins.

A second possible explanation for any discrepancy between your self-analysis and that of the exercises is that many people find it extremely difficult to isolate their feelings. Still others do not think of even having preferences for particular ways of collecting or processing data.

A third possible explanation might be that one or more of your own preferences are unclear to you. This may be due to the fact that your job or personal relationships require that you operate in a type other than your own. Over time these adopted behaviors tend to be confused with your natural preferences.

Additional Notes on Jung's Typology

Jung's typology is a descriptive theory of the different experiences that underlie behavior in normal personalities. The theory asserts that people respond differently to the same stimuli because their attitudes and functional preferences differ. These different personality types are the result of the individual's preferences for certain paired functions and for a preferred attitude. Behavior represents the collection of data through a preferred perception function, the making of decisions about that same data through a preferred judgment function, and the approach and treatment of the tasks or decision through a preferred attitude.

Jung's theory of type helps to delineate differences among personalities. It does not diagnose pathologies or evaluate a person's adjustment to reality. Instead, the theory offers behavioral descriptions of different personality types with reasons for the variations. It demonstrates that a person of a particular type will have certain predictable tendencies and resources, certain orientations to tasks, to time and to space, and that these will be shared with persons of similar type.

What each person does with these tendencies is determined by his own experiential make-up and genetic background. Any personality type can include persons who are self-confident, insecure, depressed, happy, outgoing, productive, lethargic, etc.

Furthermore, no individual displays all of the characteristics of any particular psychological type, nor do the characteristics of a particular type explain all behaviors. Environmental, cultural, and inherited characteristics invariably modify personality types. Whereas all modes of behavior are choices for each type, some behaviors are more comfortable, or natural, for one type than for the others. For example, psychological type need not determine one's choice of a profession or job. Any career is accessible to any type. Yet certain types tend to gravitate to certain types of work or careers. Thinking types tend to predominate in higher levels of teaching, management and research. Feeling types surface in the helping professions, human services, public relations, and sales. Sensors are drawn to business, production, construction, and mechanical operations. Intuitives, often indifferent to the practical side of life, prefer occupations that address ideas, possibilities, abstractions, have a minimum number of rules to follow, and call for creative or artistic expression.

Cultural and social expectations sometimes disguise and thwart an individual's typology. In a sense we are all taught to act in certain ways at certain times. In the business and academic world thinking behaviors are valued most. Young feeling, sensing, and intuitive types have learned to operate in the thinking mode in order to succeed in school or at work, saving their preferred modes for what they really enjoy most afterwards.

Understanding and accepting our types are important for reaching our potential and for having a fulfilling life. Neurosis inevitably results when our superior functions are consistently repressed or are not valued by family or immediate society. Excessive repression often leads to mental illness. Mental health and positive learning orientations demand that we be able to call on the required functions for the task at hand. Such control, the result of exercising the different functions in approved environments (home and school), provides the student with a solid basis for reaching his potential.

We each have access to all four functions and to both attitudes. Each of us thinks, senses, feels, and intuits. The more we are able to exercise the four functions, the more integrated or individuated we become as persons. The drive for wholeness is poignantly illustrated in Baum's now classic tale of the Wizard of Oz. Dorothy's trip to the Land of Oz represents the symbolic journey we undertake in an effort to become whole and human. Health and wholeness come as a result of developing, appreciating, and integrating each of the four functions within us. For example, the Scarecrow wants a brain in order to think. The Tin Man wants a heart in order to feel. The Lion wants courage which represents sensing and the need to be in control of one's environment. And the Wizard, the visionary, represents the intuitive that urges us to become all that is in us to be.

Still another way to learn about the functions is to look at an apple. This is a fruit common to us all, yet perceived differently by each. For example, the feeling function is at work in the selection of the particular apple you want to eat. The senses are working full force in telescoping messages of shape, size, weight, texture, taste, temperature, etc. The thinking function tells you the apple is good, that it is a nutritious food substance, that certain amounts of fresh fruit are necessary to a balanced diet, etc. The intuition has been hard at work all this time on a preconscious level suggesting what the apple really represents, e.g., favor in the teacher's eyes, an invitation to hidden knowledge, many different kinds of apples and their sweet differences, apples as symbols, and apples as colors, shapes, and sizes for artistic representation.[*]

*Adapted from Anna Nuernberger and Gordon Lawrence, Personality Influences in Teaching and Learning.

Summary

All four functions are inherent in each of us. We all sense, intuit, think and feel. The possession of all four functions is essential to the potential for wholeness. Yet because of environmental, familial, cultural and biological influences, we develop a preference for one of the perception functions and for one of the judgment functions.

You may find it useful to come back to the exercises in this chapter after spending some time in reflection and contemplation. Most people find the identification of the functions and types useful only after a good deal of examination and self-reflection. Self-knowledge is a slow and difficult process. The search is its own reward.

5

CHAPTER FIVE

Understanding Myself As A Learner

Introduction

In this chapter you will be asked to complete a pair of warm-up activities, "Describing Learning Experiences" and "Ten Things I Know About Myself as a Learner." These activities are designed to introduce you to the process of self-analysis and to focus your thinking on who you are as a learner. You will also be given an opportunity to identify your dominant, sub-dominant, tertiary, and inferior learning styles and to analyze your learning style profile utilizing the Learning Style Inventory. You will have an opportunity to compare your self-perceptions (regarding your preferred learning styles) with your Learning Style Inventory results by examining and ranking characterizations of the four basic learning styles. At the end of the chapter, we have included a series of questions to assist you in analyzing the data obtained from the activities, and for looking at some of the implications for teaching and learning. If we as teachers are to achieve the goal of improved decision-making, a major step is to be able to identify and respond to student learning styles. One place to begin is with ourselves as learners. If we are to be sensitive to others, we first need to become sensitive to ourselves. We need to become sensitive to our own preferences for the ways in which we, as individuals, teach and learn. We must know how these preferences affect our attitudes and behaviors in the classroom.

The activities in this chapter are designed to assist teachers in surfacing pertinent data on their own learning processes. Understanding begins with an exploration of our own psychic property, our experiences, our thoughts, and especially our feelings about who we are and how we function as learners.

WARM-UP ACTIVITIES

Activity #1: Describing Learning Experiences
The following questions are designed to assist you in your self-discovery as a learner. As you think through these questions, try to be as specific and descriptive as you can.

Questions to think about:

1. Think of two significant or rewarding learning experiences you have had. Describe these experiences in the manual, in a log or diary, or on a tape recorder. What was it about each experience that made it important to you?

Description of experience 1

_____

_____

_____

_____

Importance to me

_____

_____

_____

_____

_____

Description of experience 2

_____

_____

_____

_____

_____

Importance to me

_____

_____

_____

_____

_____

2. What was common to both of these experiences?

_____

_____

_____

_____

3. How did you feel about each of these experiences? Can you think of any reasons which account for these feelings?

_____

_____

_____

_____

_____

4. Now, for a change of pace, think of a body of content, a task, or a skill that you have had (or are having) difficulty learning. What was it? Describe the experience.

_____

_____

_____

_____

_____

_____

_____

_____

_____

_____

5. What was (is) it about this experience that made it difficult?

_____

_____

_____

_____

_____

_____

_____

_____

_____

_____

6. What would have been a better way for you to have learned this difficult material? Describe some of the steps you might take.

_____

_____

_____

_____

_____

_____

_____

_____

_____

_____

Activity #2: Ten Things I Know About Myself as a Learner

Reflect for a moment on what you know about yourself as a learner. Then, list ten things you know about how you learn. Write down whatever comes to mind. Begin each statement with I. Please be as specific as you can. (The columns at the right of the form are for later use.)

Learner Behaviors	Content	Physical condition	Psychological condition	Process	Activities	Mode
1. I _____						
2. I _____						
3. I _____						
4. I _____						
5. I _____						
6. I _____						
7. I _____						
8. I _____						
9. I _____						
10. I _____						

Read the six categories across the top of the "Ten Things I Know About Myself as a Learner" worksheet. The definitions below are provided for your assistance.

Content: kinds of information, things, ideas, and subject matter learned, such as technical material, art forms, social issues, history, theories, or facts.

Physical Conditions: the physical environment most conducive to learning, including such things as lighting, noise level, temperature, furniture, space, mobility, etc.

Psychological Conditions: the psychological environment most conducive to learning, including personal motivations, interactions with others, ego needs, and trust

Process: the steps involved in learning, including note-taking, memorizing, talking to experts, analyzing, constructing, comparing, contrasting, etc.

Activities: the method of delivery, such as reading, lectures, multimedia, workbooks, or field trips

Mode: the method of data reception including auditory, visual, kinesthetic, taste, and smell

Having reviewed the six categories, go back now and fill in each column as it may relate to your learning statements. You may feel that some of the category definitions fit more than one learning behavior. That is perfectly acceptable. Other learning behaviors may have no corollary definitions. The point of the "Ten Things" exercise is to get you to describe as completely as you can the total circumstances behind your learning statements.

Analyze your statements now by considering the following questions:

What types or kinds of things most interest me?

_____

_____

_____

_____

Under what conditions, physical and psychological, do I learn best?

_____

_____

_____

_____

What conditions make it difficult for me to learn?

_____

_____

_____

_____

What activities, processes, and modes of learning do I prefer?

_____

_____

_____

_____

_____

What two behaviors, from my list of ten, are most important for my success as a learner? (Try to think of personal examples for these two learning behaviors that you consider most important.)

_____

_____

_____

_____

_____

What information do I have about myself that a teacher, instructor or friend should know about me in order to work with me more successfully?

_____

_____

_____

_____

_____

In order to bring together all of this information, complete the following statements: I learn best when…

_____

_____

_____

_____

It is difficult for me to learn when…

_____

_____

_____

_____

_____

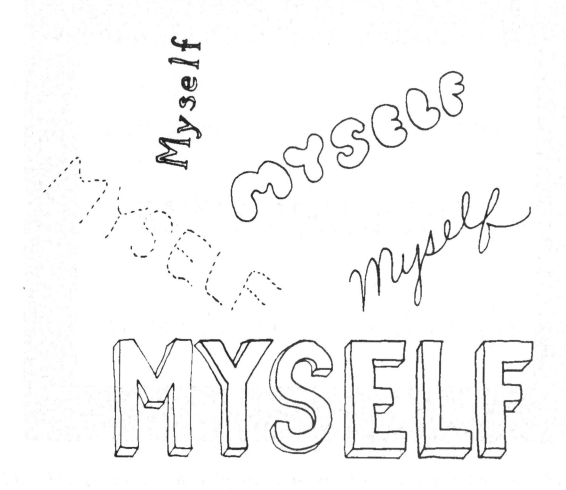

The Learning Style Inventory

The first set of activities were designed to introduce you to the process of self-analysis and to stimulate your thinking about your learning behaviors in preparation for examining your preferred learning styles. In this section, an additional focusing step will be taken as you look at your learning behaviors in light of

Jung's theories applied to learning preferences.

The Learning Style Inventory (LSI) is a simple self-descriptive instrument designed to help you identify your own learning style and profile, i.e., what styles you depend on (dominant); use often (sub-dominant); don't use often (tertiary); or rarely ever use (inferior).

A LEARNING STYLE INVENTORY FOR ADULTS

A self-diagnostic tool for adults to use in identifying their learning style and profile based on Carl Gustav Jung's Theory of Psychological Types

Developed by
Harvey F. Silver and J. Robert Hanson
Revised November, 1998

Silver Strong & Associates, Inc.
The Thoughtful Education Press
1-800-962-4432

I. CHOOSING SELF DESCRIPTORS

In each of the following twenty-five horizontal sets, rank the four behavioral descriptors in order of: first preference (5), second preference (3), third preference (1), fourth preference (0).

Be sure to assign a different weighted number (5,3,1,0) to each of the four descriptors in each set. Do not make ties. Rank the descriptors according to those which best describe you, i.e., how you approach learning. Note that a rank of zero does not mean a descriptor does not apply to you; it only means that descriptor is your least preferred.

Please answer every item and keep in mind that there are no right or wrong answers. The aim of this inventory is to describe how you learn, not to evaluate your learning ability or to assign labels. If a set of words is hard to rank at first reading, then go to the next set. Complete the missing set after you've finished all the other items.

> Descriptors are to be analyzed horizontally as sets of four across the lettered columns.
> Do not compare descriptors vertically.

	A	B	C	D
1.	Creative	Personal	Organized	Analytical
2.	Facts	Formulas	Passions	People
3.	Spontaneous	Flexible	Literal	Interpretive
4.	Harmonize	Question	Utilize	Imagine
5.	Create	Compete	Cooperate	Critique
6.	Remember	Reason	Relate Personally	Reorganize
7.	Discovery	Debate	Directions	Discussion
8.	Patterns	Human Interactions	Details	Possibilities
9.	Feelings	Objects	Ideas	Insights
10.	Action	Wonder	Warmth	Wisdom
11.	Eureka!	Trial & Error	Gut Feeling	Strategy
12.	Realistic	Theoretical	Aesthetic	Humanistic
13.	Specifics	Concepts	Values	Rapport
14.	Logic	Precision	Persuasion	Predictions
15.	Knowing	Relating	Expressing	Understanding
16.	Idealize	Systematize	Socialize	Routinize
17.	Intellectual	Compassionate	Pragmatic	Idealistic
18.	Invention	Intimacy	Information	Inquiry
19.	Loyalties	Rules	Principles	Metaphors
20.	Inspirational	Logical	Experiential	Methodical
21.	Argument	Accuracy	Affiliation	Alternatives
22.	Clarity	Curiosity	Empathy	Originality
23.	Explanation	Extrapolation	Emulation	Example
24.	Enthusiasm	Experience	Effort	Examination
25.	Symmetrical	Sequential	Scientific	Social

II. JUNG'S THEORY OF PERSONALITY TYPE

How we learn is a fascinating and individual process. As Carl Jung discovered, any learning process requires both *perception* — how we find out about persons, places, and things — and *judgment* — how we process or make judgments about what we perceive. Perception occurs in one of two ways (called functions), either by "sensing" or "intuiting." Judgment also occurs in one of two ways, either by "thinking" or "feeling." Behaviors associated with each function are outlined in Table 1.

Table 1: The Four Functions

Perception Functions		Judgment Functions	
Sensing	**Intuiting**	**Thinking**	**Feeling**
Prefers action to wonder	Prefers wonder to action	Prefers to make decisions based on logical analysis	Prefers to make decisions based on personal feelings
Prefers a standard way of doing things	Prefers own way of doing things	Thinks things through before taking action	Responds to feelings and is spontaneous
Interested in activities that have immediate, practical use	Interested in activities that generate possibilities and go beyond what is	Decides independently of others	Seeks approval of others before making a decision
Works steadily when given a realistic idea of how long a task will take	Works in bursts of energy powered by enthusiasm	Needs to be right and treated fairly	Needs to be liked and treated in a friendly manner
More comfortable with concrete details than abstract ideas	More comfortable with abstract ideas than concrete details	Responds to logic and reason	Responds to own likes and dislikes and other people's reactions

The preference for sensing or intuition is independent of the preference for thinking or feeling. As a result, four distinct combinations occur. These combinations are called learning styles.

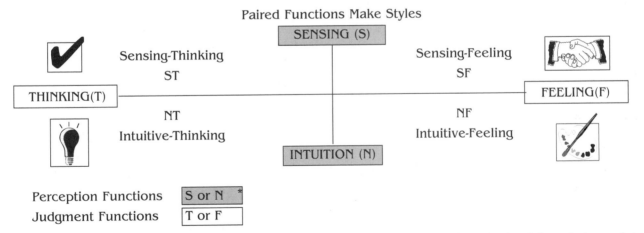

Paired Functions Make Styles

Each of these combinations produces a different kind of learning style characterized by whatever interests, values, needs, habits of mind, surface traits, and learning behaviors naturally result from these combinations. Descriptions of the four learning styles appear on pages 4-5.

*"N" is used for "intuition" since, in the larger profile, "I" is used for "introversion."

Understanding Myself As A Learner

III. SUBJECTIVE RANKING

Before scoring your learning profile, please rank order the styles based on your own immediate perceptions of your learning needs and preferences. Please carefully read the style descriptions which follow and determine which description is most characteristic, next most characteristic, third most, and least characteristic.

Sensing-Thinking Learners (ST)

Overview: Realistic, practical, and matter-of-fact.

Sensing Thinkers are efficient and results-oriented, preferring action to words and involvement to theory. They have a high energy level for doing things which are pragmatic, logical, and useful.

Approach to Learning

Sensing-Thinking learners like to complete their work in an organized and efficient manner. They tend to be neat, well-organized, and precise in their work. They have an appetite for work, need to be kept busy, and require immediate feedback. They would rather do almost anything than remain in their seat listening to someone speak. They need to be active, to be doing, to see tangible results from their efforts, and to be in control of the task.

Sensing-Thinking learners prefer step-by-step directions when assigned a task and become impatient if the instructions become long and involved. More than any other learner, they want to know exactly what is expected of them. They need to know what they have to do, how they are to do it, and when it is to be done. Sensing-Thinking learners will often lose interest in an activity if it moves too slowly, or if they can see no practical use for it.

Sensing-Thinking learners need clearly-structured environments focusing on factual mastery of skills and an opportunity to apply them to something practical or to demonstrate proficiency in the skill. They prefer assignments which have right or wrong responses rather than open-ended or interpretive ones. They are highly motivated by competition, learning games, grades, gold stars, etc.

Intuitive-Thinking Learners (NT)

Overview: Theoretical, intellectual, and knowledge-oriented.

Intuitive Thinkers prefer to be challenged intellectually and to think things through for themselves. They are curious about ideas, have a tolerance for theory, a taste for complex problems, and a concern for long-range consequences.

Approach to Learning

Intuitive-Thinking learners approach learning in a logical, organized, systematic fashion, bringing organization and structure to people and things. They take time to plan, organize ideas, and determine necessary resources before beginning work on an assignment.

Intuitive Thinkers prefer to work independently or with other thinking types and require little feedback until their work is completed. They do not like to be pressed for time. When working on something of interest, time is meaningless. They display a great deal of patience and persistence in completing difficult assignments if the assignment has captured their interest.

Intuitive Thinkers attack problems by breaking them down into their component parts. They like to reason things out and to look for logical relationships. Their thought processes follow a cause-and-effect line of reasoning. They are constantly asking "why?" and their questions tend to be provocative. Their concern is for relevance and meaning.

Intuitive Thinkers are avid readers. Their learning is vicarious, and therefore, abstract symbols, formulae, the written word, and technical illustrations are preferred sources for collecting data.

Intuitive Thinkers usually display a facility for language and express their ideas in detail. Everything they touch turns into words, spoken or written. They enjoy arguing a point based on logical analysis. In discussion, they often play the role of "devil's advocate" or purposefully argue an opposite point of view.

Intuitive Thinkers are also concerned about being correct. They strive towards perfection, are self-critical, and are upset by mistakes—their own or other people's.

Intuitive-Feeling Learners (NF)

Overview: Curious, insightful, and imaginative.

Intuitive Feelers are the ones who dare to dream, are committed to their values, are open to alternatives, and are constantly searching for new and unusual ways to express themselves.

Approach to Learning

Intuitive-Feeling students approach learning eager to explore ideas, generate new solutions to problems, and discuss moral dilemmas. Their interests are varied and unpredictable, but they prefer activities which allow them to use their imaginations and do things in unique ways. They are turned off by routine or rote assignments and prefer questions which are open ended, such as "What would happen if…?"

Intuitive Feelers are highly motivated by their own interests. Things of interest will be done inventively well. Things which they do not like may be done poorly or forgotten altogether. When engaged in a project which intrigues them, time is meaningless. Intuitive Feelers operate by an "internal clock" and, therefore, often feel constrained or frustrated by external rules or schedules.

Intuitive Feelers are independent and non-conforming. They do not fear being different and are usually aware of their own and others' impulses. They are open to the irrational and not confined by convention. They are sensitive to beauty and symmetry and will comment on the aesthetic characteristics of things.

Intuitive Feelers prefer not to follow step-by-step procedures but rather to move where their intuitions take them. They prefer to find their own solutions rather than being told what to do or how to do it. They are able to take intuitive leaps, and they trust their own insights. Intuitive Feelers often take circuitous routes to solving problems and may not be able to explain how they arrived at the answer.

Highly adaptable to new situations, Intuitive Feelers are flexible in thought and action. They prefer dynamic environments with many resources and materials. Intuitive Feelers, more than any other type, are less likely to be disturbed by changes in routine. They are comfortable working with a minimum of directions. Their work is sometimes scattered and may look chaotic to thinking types. Intuitive-Feeling learners are often engaged in a number of activities at the same time and move from one to the other according to where their interests take them. Often, they start more projects than they can finish.

Sensing-Feeling Learners (SF)

Overview: Sociable, friendly, and interpersonally-oriented.

Sensing-Feeling learners are sensitive to people's feelings—their own and others'. They prefer to learn about things that directly affect people's lives rather than impersonal facts or theories.

Approach to Learning

Sensing Feelers take a personal approach to learning. They work best when emotionally involved in what they are being asked to learn. Sensing-Feeling learners tend to be spontaneous and often act on impulse, i.e., in terms of what "feels right." They are interested in people and like to listen to and talk about people and their feelings. They like to be helpful to others and need to be recognized for their efforts.

Sensing-Feeling learners, more than any other type, enjoy personal attention. They need to feel relaxed, comfortable, and to enjoy themselves while they learn. They like to think out loud, to work with other students, to share their ideas, and to get the reactions of their friends. They much prefer cooperation to competition, and they need reassurance or praise that lets them know they are doing well. They are greatly influenced by the likes and dislikes of others. On occasion, they may complete a task as a means of pleasing someone rather than because they are interested in the task itself.

SUBJECTIVE RANKING PREFERENCES

1. Most characteristic_____

3. Third most characteristic_____

2. Second most characteristic_____

4. Least characteristic _____

Understanding Myself As A Learner

IV. ASSESSING YOUR ABILITIES

Having subjectively ranked your learning styles, read the descriptions of learning abilities by style. Identify those abilities you feel you would like to develop with a check (3). Identify your strongest abilities with a plus sign (+).

ST ABILITIES	SF ABILITIES
— good at working with and remembering facts and details — able to speak and write directly to the point — approach tasks in an organized and sequential manner — adapt to existing procedures and guidelines — concerned with utility and efficiency — goal-oriented; focus on immediate, tangible outcomes — know what needs to be done and follow through — concerned with accuracy	— spontaneous and open to impulses; do what feels good — able to express personal feelings — aware of others' feelings and make judgments based on personal likes and dislikes — learn through human interaction and personal experience — comfortable with activities requiring the expression of feelings — able to persuade people through personal interaction — keen observers of human nature — interested in people and act on their behalf
NT ABILITIES	**NF ABILITIES**
— take time to plan and contemplate consequences of actions — able to organize and synthesize information — weigh the evidence and make judgments based on logic — learn vicariously through books and other symbolic forms — comfortable with activities requiring logical analysis — able to persuade people through logical analysis — retain and recall large amounts of knowledge and information — interested in ideas, theories, or concepts	— good at interpreting facts and details to see the broader picture — able to express ideas in new and unusual ways — approach tasks in a variety of ways or in an exploratory manner — adapt to new situations and procedures quickly — concerned with beauty, symmetry, and form — process-oriented; interested in the future and solving problems of human welfare — concerned with creativity

Now that you have subjectively ranked your styles and assessed your abilities, you are ready to compute your learning score. Follow the directions on the following pages for computing your learning score and completing your learning profile. Then, compare your personal analysis of your learning profile with the profile indicated by your score.

V. SCORING SELF DESCRIPTORS

To compute your learning score for each of the four learning styles, first remove the insert sheet, (pp.3 through 6), then transfer the numbers from your answer sheet to the scoring sheet. For example, if in the first set of behaviors, you ranked the words as

1. <u>0</u> Creative   <u>5</u> Personal   <u>3</u> Organized   <u>1</u> Analytical

then transfer these same numbers to the same words on the scoring sheet, as follows:

1. <u>5</u> Personal   <u>3</u> Organized   <u>1</u> Analytical   <u>0</u> Creative

Compute your scores by adding the numbers for each column vertically.

S-F Style Sensing-Feeling Rank	S-T Style Sensing-Thinking Rank	N-T Style Intuitive-Thinking Rank	N-F Style Intuitive-Feeling Rank
1. ____Personal	____Organized	____Analytical	____Creative
2. ____People	____Facts	____Formulas	____Passions
3. ____Spontaneous	____Literal	____Interpretive	____Flexible
4. ____Harmonize	____Utilize	____Question	____Imagine
5. ____Cooperate	____Compete	____Critique	____Create
6. ____Relate Personally	____Remember	____Reason	____Reorganize
7. ____Discussion	____Directions	____Debate	____Discovery
8. ____Human Interactions	____Details	____Patterns	____Possibilities
9. ____Feelings	____Objects	____Ideas	____Insights
10. ____Warmth	____Action	____Wisdom	____Wonder
11. ____Gut Feeling	____Trial & Error	____Strategy	____Eureka!
12. ____Humanistic	____Realistic	____Theoretical	____Aesthetic
13. ____Rapport	____Specifics	____Concepts	____Values
14. ____Persuasion	____Precision	____Logic	____Predictions
15. ____Relating	____Knowing	____Understanding	____Expressing
16. ____Socialize	____Routinize	____Systematize	____Idealize
17. ____Compassionate	____Pragmatic	____Intellectual	____Idealistic
18. ____Intimacy	____Information	____Inquiry	____Invention
19. ____Loyalties	____Rules	____Principles	____Metaphors
20. ____Experiential	____Methodical	____Logical	____Inspirational
21. ____Affiliation	____Accuracy	____Argument	____Alternatives
22. ____Empathy	____Clarity	____Curiosity	____Originality
23. ____Emulation	____Example	____Explanation	____Extrapolation
24. ____Experience	____Effort	____Examination	____Enthusiasm
25. ____Social	____Sequential	____Scientific	____Symmetrical

TOTALS

SF _____   ST _____   NT _____   NF _____

     Understanding Myself As A Learner

VI. ANALYZING YOUR LEARNING PREFERENCES

STRENGTHS OF THE PREFERENCES

100 - 125	Very strong choice; very comfortable in the style
75 - 99	Strong choice; comfortable in the style
50 - 74	Moderate choice
25 - 49	Low comfort in the style
0 - 24	Very low comfort in the style

LEARNING PROFILE

No one learning style adequately represents the complexity of one's learning behavior. Everyone operates in a variety of ways in different situations. Depending on how demanding a particular learning challenge may be, one "flexes" or compensates by using other, often less-preferred, styles. It's important, therefore, to identify not just one's dominant or most-accessible style, but also one's entire profile. It is the full profile that gives the only accurate picture of how one functions. One's profile consists of four styles in a descending order of access. The dominant style is the most accessible because it is the most practiced. The auxiliary style is accessible with some additional effort. The third level (tertiary) and least developed (inferior) are such because they are not routinely practiced and therefore, are much less accessible. One's profile is always a hierarchy, but over time and with increasing consciousness, the tertiary and inferior functions can become more accessible as a result of practice.

MODE	SCORE	STYLE	COMFORT LEVEL (top, p.62)	SUBJECTIVE RANKING (bottom, p.59)
Dominant				
Auxiliary				
Tertiary				
Inferior				

DIRECTIONS FOR PLOTTING YOUR LEARNING PROFILE:

Having completed the scoring of your learning styles, plot your profile below. To plot your profile, mark the score you received for each style on the diagonal line that fits that style. Then connect your marks with a straight line to create a four-sided polygon. This configuration represents a visual presentation of your learning profile.

VISUAL PRESENTATION OF MY LEARNING PROFILE

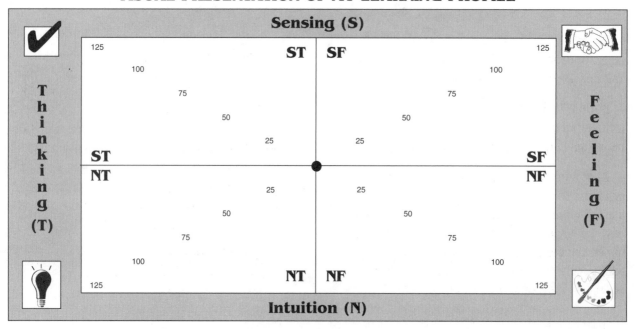

Characterizations of Learning Styles

Having completed and analyzed your learning profile, you will be asked to rank the descriptions of the four basic learning styles. Read through each of the four descriptions and rank them according to the one which is most characteristic of you as a learner (dominant learning style), second most characteristic (sub-dominant learning style), third most characteristic (tertiary learning style), and least like you (inferior learning style). Before you read the descriptions and perform the ranking task some interpretive or precautionary notes are in order.

First, the following descriptions are characterizations. They are written in generalities to provide mental pictures of the four learning styles. As such they are stereotypes, and no one is exactly like the learner described.

As you read the descriptions, you will find that one style may be "right on target" except for a few words or phrases. We suggest that you focus on the appropriateness of the description in its totality as a self-indicator rather than on the points that may be atypical.

Second, each learning style reflects aspects of your behavior. Certainly some styles are more reflective of your perceived behaviors than others. There may be one style with which you have little or no compatibility.

Third, no one style or combination of styles is better than any other. Each style has its own assets and liabilities.

Fourth, learning preferences are heavily influenced by environment. Thus, our styles may be influenced as the environment changes.

Last, for some of us it is easier to find our dominant style, and for others it is easier to identify the least-used style. In either event you will now have some new verbal pegs on which to "hang" a better understanding of how you function as a learner. In addition, these sensitivities will assist you in more accurately assessing how others may learn.

Interpreting the Learning Style Inventory

Still another way to interpret the LSI's findings is to look at the dominant and sub-dominant choices in terms of either the judgment or perception functions. The chances are that either the perception or the judgment functions will be the same for both the first and second choices. For example, if your dominant was Sensing-Thinking and your auxiliary was Intuitive-Thinking, then in both cases you prefer thinking as the judgment mode. This choice also means that feeling is the least preferred and falls therefore in the "tertiary" and "inferior" categories. Or, conversely, if both perception functions fall in the dominant auxiliary choices, then the opposite perception function is clearly relegated to the supportive and least-used categories, e.g., where dominant Sensing-Feeling is paired with auxiliary Sensing-Thinking the clear preference is for sensing as the perception mechanism. Intuition is, therefore, the third and last choice.

The Sensing-Feeling Learner

*Overview**

The Sensing-Feeling learner can be characterized as sociable, friendly, and inter-personally oriented. This type of learner is very sensitive to people's feelings; his own and others'. He prefers to learn about things that directly affect people's lives rather than impersonal facts or theories.

Approach To Learning

The Sensing-Feeler's approach to learning is a personal one. He works best when emotionally involved in what he is being asked to learn. The Sensing-Feeling learner tends to be spontaneous and often acts on impulse, i.e., in terms of what "feels right." He is interested in people and likes to listen to and talk about people and their feelings. He likes to be helpful to others and needs to be recognized for his efforts.

*For the purposes of describing behaviors we are following the convention of referring to teachers using the female pronoun, and to students using the male pronoun.

The Sensing-Feeling learner, more than any other type, enjoys personal attention. He needs to feel relaxed, comfortable, and to enjoy himself while he learns. He likes to think out loud, to work with other students, to share his ideas, and to get the reactions of his friends. He much prefers cooperation to competition and needs reassurance or praise that he is doing well. He is greatly influenced by the likes and dislikes of others. On occasion he may complete an assignment more to please someone else than because of any interest he has in the task itself.

Approach To Problem-Solving

The Sensing-Feeler's approach to problem-solving activities is greatly influenced by his own values and life experiences. He may disregard or reject information that does not conform to his own life experiences. He likes harmony and prefers to work in group situations as a way to draw out pertinent facts for problem-solving. He is comfortable working with interpersonal problems because of his sensitivity to people's feelings.

Assets And Liabilities

The Sensing-Feeling learner's strength is his interest in other people. He is sensitive to his own and others' concerns and will listen to many different points of view. He works best in group situations and knows what it takes to facilitate group movement and growth. He is trusted by others because he is spontaneous, shows emotion, and is honest about his feelings.

On the other hand, the Sensing-Feeler learner has liabilities. Because he is so involved with his feelings, he is easily hurt by others and may be overemotional. He finds it difficult to separate himself from his work and takes constructive criticism as an attack on his personal self-worth. He may be so concerned with what other people think and feel that he is unable to assert himself, to express his own opinions, to stand firm for what he believes, to take charge, or to lead. He often finds it difficult to plan ahead and to be objective, or to weight the evidence around him before he takes action on his feelings.

Learns Best

The Sensing-Feeler learns best in a warm, friendly, supportive, and interactive environment in which students are encouraged to share their personal thoughts, feelings, and experiences, and to interact with one another.

He benefits most when the instructional process emphasizes collaborative approaches in which students share ideas and materials and work in small groups.

The Sensing-Feeler thinks best when talking and/or listening to other people. It is often difficult for him to sit down and begin work, especially when it does not relate to him personally, or when it has to be done alone.

The Sensing-Feeler enjoys group activities, games with lots action in which everyone can participate and no one loses, discussions, reading stories about people and their feelings, writing and talking about things he likes to do, group process activities, and art and music, which allow him to express his feelings.

The Sensing-Feeling student needs to participate in group activities to develop his power of empathy. He needs to have time and resources to learn about himself. He needs to have an opportunity to explore, change, and develop attitudes and values in reference to others.

The Sensing-Feeling student learns best from first hand experiences that relate to him personally and help him to understand who he is and how he functions.

The Sensing-Feeling student enjoys working with others and is particularly sensitive to their approval or disapproval. He is equally sensitive to indifference. He is influenced more by his peers than by authority figures and may lose sight of his own ideas while trying to cooperate with the group.

The Sensing-Feeling learner views content mastery as secondary to achieving harmonious relationships with others. He enjoys learning through group process, personal friendships, and tender (if not loving) attention.

Most of all, the Sensing-Feeling learner is a verbal learner. They need to be able to talk, to ask questions, and to interact with their peers. They do not do well when forced to listen. While they are auditory learners their ability to listen is directly correlated to their verbal involvement. For the SF the thinking organizational task is done by speaking, by trying out ideas, by asking "foolish" questions. The SF learns best in small groups, dyads, and pair/share settings.

The Sensing-Thinking Learner

Overview

The Sensing-Thinking learner can be characterized as realistic, practical, and matter-of-fact. This type of learner is efficient and results-oriented.

He prefers action to words and involvement to theory. He has a high energy level for doing things which are pragmatic, logical, and useful.

Approach To Learning

The Sensing-Thinking learner likes to complete his work in an organized and efficient manner. He tends to be neat, well-organized and precise in his work. His appetite for work and his need for immediate feedback is often a challenge for the teacher. The Sensing-Thinking learner enjoys work and needs to be kept busy. He would rather do almost anything than remain in his seat listening to someone speak. He needs to be active, to be doing, to see tangible results from his efforts, and to be in control of the task.

The Sensing-Thinking learner prefers step-by-step directions when assigned a task and becomes impatient if the instructions become long and involved.

More than any other learner, this type wants to know exactly what is expected of him. He needs to know what he is to do, how well he is to do it, and when it is to be done. The Sensing-Thinking learner will often lose interest in an activity if it moves too slowly, or if he can see no practical use for it.

The Sensing-Thinking learner needs clearly structured environments with the main focus on factual mastery of skills and an opportunity to apply them to something practical or to demonstrate proficiency in the skill. He prefers assignments which have right or wrong responses rather than open-ended or interpretive ones. He is highly motivated by competition, learning games, grades, gold stars, etc.

Approach To Problem-Solving

The Sensing-Thinker's approach to problem-solving emphasizes specific facts, trial and error, and pragmatic solutions. Problems are seen as puzzles that require constant manipulation of the pieces until the correct solution is discovered. The Sensing-Thinker works best with problems that require concrete exploration and manipulation rather than the analysis of abstractions. When confronted with a problem, he looks for solutions from past experiences and relies on previously tested procedures rather than looking for new solutions. If the first attempt at a solution

doesn't work, he will try another—as long as time and resources permit. Sensing-Thinkers are people of action searching for practical solutions to their immediate problems.

Assets And Liabilities

The Sensing-Thinker's strengths are in his ability to apply himself to the task at hand. He is concerned with action and tangible results. He is highly task-oriented and a good person to have on a committee concerned about getting work done. He is organized, adept at collecting the facts, and attentive to detail. He is pragmatic and able to apply past experience to problems. He searches for simple yet workable solutions and is able to face difficulty with realism. He is able to write and speak directly to the point. He is efficient and tends not to procrastinate.

On the other hand, the Sensing-Thinking learner's liabilities are that he may be inflexible and unable to adapt to change. He may be dogmatic and headstrong. He has a limited tolerance for ambiguity and thus may take action before he has considered all the

consequences. The Sensing-Thinking learner may oversimplify complex issues or fail to see the possibilities beyond the immediate facts. He is overly concerned about what is right and wrong so that he overlooks the gray areas where truth tends to lurk. He distrusts those things which can't be quickly verified by the senses. Because of his task orientation, he may overlook the feelings of the people with whom he is working.

Learns Best

The Sensing-Thinker learns best in an organized, systematic, activity-oriented, instructor-directed atmosphere. He needs to be actively engaged in purposeful work. The instructional environment requires well-defined procedures and content. This content needs to be presented in an orderly and systematic manner. The instructional emphases for the Sensing-Thinker are on convergent, competitive, and independent approaches to learning.

The Sensing-Thinker learns best when he can directly experience with his five senses what he is expected to learn. Motivation comes from being able to see the practicality of what he has learned and from putting the new learning into immediate use. Thus, the Sensing-Thinker learns best when he can see the utility of what he is asked to learn. (Sometimes the need for utility can be alternatively satisfied by good grades or other tangible forms of recognition).

The Sensing-Thinking learner has little tolerance for ambiguous situations. He wants to know what is expected of him before he begins. He needs clearly stated ground rules. He works best when there are clearly stated objectives and when achievement is quickly recognized and rewarded.

The Sensing-Thinking learner likes games that have competition, clear rules, and lots of action.

The Sensing-Thinking learner needs a clearly defined instructional approach with the focus on content mastery, the mastery of basic skills, or the immediate opportunity to employ what has been learned. He learns best from repetition, drill, memorization, programmed instruction, workbooks, demonstration, field trips, and direct actual experience. In short, he needs well-defined action activities and immediate tangible results.

The Intuitive-Thinking Learner

Overview

The Intuitive-Thinking learner can be characterized as theoretical, intellectual, and knowledge-oriented. This type of learner prefers to be challenged intellectually and to think things through for himself. The Intuitive-Thinker is curious about ideas, has a tolerance for theory, a taste for complex problems, and a concern for long-range consequences.

Approach To Learning

The Intuitive-Thinking learner approaches schoolwork in a logical, organized, systematic fashion. The Intuitive-Thinker brings organization and structure to both people and things. He takes time to plan and think things through before beginning work on assignment. He organizes his ideas and determines what resources are necessary to complete required tasks.

The Intuitive-Thinker prefers to work independently or with other thinking types. He requires little feedback until his work is completed. He does not like to be pressed for time. When working on something of interest, time is meaningless. He displays a great deal of patience and persistence in completing difficult assignments if they have captured his interest.

The Intuitive-Thinking learner's approach to understanding things and ideas is by breaking them down into their component parts. He likes to reason things out and to look for logical relationships. His thought processes follow a cause-and-effect line of reasoning. He is constantly asking "why?" His questions tend to be provocative as compared to questions about information or facts. His concern is for relevance and meaning.

The Intuitive-Thinker is an avid reader. His learning is vicarious, and therefore abstract symbols, formulae, the written word, and technical illustrations are preferred sources for collecting data.

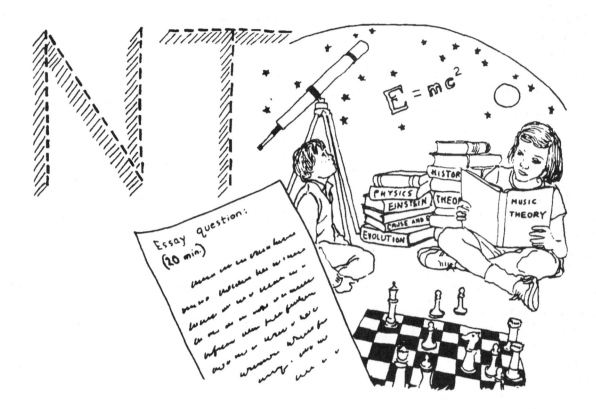

The Intuitive-Thinker usually displays a facility for language and expresses his ideas in detail. Everything the Intuitive-Thinker touches turns into words, spoken or written. He enjoys arguing a point based on logical analysis. In discussion, he often enjoys the role of "devil's advocate" or purposefully arguing an opposite point of view. The dialectic method of inquiry is an NT's favorite for thorough examination of multiple points of view, not just one or two, some otherwise unattainable truth may leak through.

The Intuitive-Thinking learner is also concerned about being correct. He strives toward perfection, is self-critical, and is upset by mistakes—his own or other people's.

Approach To Problem-Solving

The Intuitive-Thinker approaches problem-solving situations with relish. He enjoys looking at the problem from as many perspectives as possible. He is precise in his formulation of the problem statement. He then looks for as many alternative solutions as are feasible in resolving the situation. He is not bothered by the complexities of the problem, and generally does not become too invested in details. His main concern is to properly conceptualize the problem issues so that he can postulate solutions. He especially enjoys the thought process that goes with looking at the cause and effect relationships for each proposed solution.

Assets And Liabilities

The Intuitive-Thinking learner sets high standards for himself and for those with whom he works. At his best, he is adept at analyzing complex ideas and theories and at discovering principles and relationships among ideas. He is objective, able to organize information, forecast consequences, weigh the law and evidence, and apply previously learned ideas to new situations. His ideas are well thought out, and he is able to stand firm against opposition. He is patient, persistent, enjoys research, and is comfortable addressing intellectually challenging problems.

On the other hand, at his worst, he may be overly critical of himself and others. When making a point, he may show a lack of concern for the feelings of others. When explaining what he knows, he will monopolize conversations by rambling on in abstractions which no one else is following. His conversations may turn into theoretical lectures. He talks above people rather than with them. He may have little tolerance for other people's ideas especially if they disagree with his own positions. He may be so involved with his own reasoning that he fails to see the reasoning of others. He may have difficulty working with others.

Learns Best

The Intuitive-Thinker learns best in an intellectually stimulating atmosphere in which he is challenged to think critically and analytically and in which he is "stretched" to increase his reasoning abilities. The instructional emphasis for the Intuitive-Thinker is placed on independent and creative approaches to learning. He prefers to learn by discovery and experimentation.

The Intuitive-Thinker learner needs to have the freedom to identify his own interests, to participate in selecting his own learning activities, and to have the time and resources to develop his own ideas. This Intuitive-Thinking learner enjoys independent research projects, reading on topics of current interest, theorizing, lectures, games of strategy, expression of ideas, debates, and projects which call for the use of critical analysis and the formulation of new ideas or elegant evaluations.

The Intuitive-Feeling Learner

Overview

The Intuitive-Feeling learner can be characterized as curious, insightful, and imaginative. The Intuitive-Feeler is one who dares to dream, is committed to his values, is open to alternatives and is constantly searching for new and unusual ways to express himself.

Approach To Learning

The Intuitive-Feeling student approaches learning eager to explore ideas, to generate new solutions to problems, and to discuss moral dilemmas. The Intuitive-Feeler's interests are varied and unpredictable. He enjoys a wide variety of things. He prefers activities which allow him to use his imagination and to do

things in new and different ways. He is turned off by routine or rote assignments and prefers questions which are open ended, such as "What would happen if…?"

The Intuitive-Feeling student is highly motivated by his own interests. Things of interest will be done inventively well. Things which he does not like may be poorly done or forgotten altogether. When engaged in a project which intrigues him, time is meaningless. The Intuitive-Feeler operates by an "internal clock" and, therefore, often feels constrained or frustrated by external rules or schedules.

The Intuitive-Feeling learner is independent and non-conforming. He does not fear being different and is usually aware of his own and other people's impulses. He is open to the irrational and not confined by convention. He is sensitive to beauty and symmetry and will comment on the aesthetic characteristics of things.

The Intuitive-Feeling learner prefers not to follow step-by-step procedures but rather to move where his intuition takes him. He prefers to find his own solutions to challenges or problems rather than being told what to do or how to do it. He is able to take intuitive leaps. He trusts his own insights. He often looks for new and different ways to solve problems. He often takes circuitous routes to get where he wants to go. He may solve a problem but not be able to explain how he arrived at his answer.

The Intuitive-Feeling learner is able to adapt to new situations. He is flexible in thought and action. He prefers changing environments with many resources and materials. The Intuitive-Feeler, more than any other type, is less likely to be disturbed by changes in routine. The Intuitive-Feeler is comfortable working with a minimum of directions. His work is sometimes scattered and may look chaotic to thinking types. The Intuitive-Feeling learner is often engaged in a number of activities at the same time and moves from one to the other according to where his interests take him. He starts more projects than he finishes.

Approach To Problem-Solving

The Intuitive-Feeler enjoys solving new problems. He is particularly interested in problems of human welfare. He is adept at thinking divergently and searching for alternative solutions. He often offers unusual, unique, inventive, or "way out" responses. He sometimes is more concerned about generating possible solutions to a problem than choosing one and carrying it out. The Intuitive-Feeler is interested in the future, "what might be," and "what could happen." He looks beyond facts and details to see the broad perspective or the "big picture." He needs to look at a problem from many different perspectives and searches for unique and unexpected solutions.

Assets And Liabilities

The Intuitive-Feeling learner is not constrained by convention and is open to new ideas and approaches. He is able to think divergently, is idealistic, and is willing to tackle difficult problems with zest. He is able to arouse enthusiasm and commitment on the part of others to achieve a goal. He is creative and adept at reading the signs of coming change, is able to supply ingenuity to problem-solving, and

is able to generate new and unusual possibilities for addressing issues of human welfare.

On the other hand, his approach to problems, though creative, is sometimes unrealistic and lacks pragmatic judgment. The Intuitive-Feeler, at his worst, has difficulty facing problems with realism. He is never satisfied with what is and always wants to change something. He moves from one good idea to another, but may be unable to put any of the ideas into action. He is enthusiastic about what he is doing one day and bored the next. He is over-committed and involves himself in many more projects than he can complete He has difficulty planning and organizing his time. He often overlooks essential details and fails to take action on what needs to be done at the moment.

Learns Best

The Intuitive-Feeler learns best in a flexible and innovative atmosphere where there are a minimum number of restrictions, many alternative activities, and where a premium is placed on creating his own learning activities or solutions to problems. The Intuitive-Feeler's instructional emphases are on curiosity,

creativity, and a clarification of his personal values. He enjoys self-expressive activities, creating things, projects designed around his own interest, reading, messy activities, meditation, contemplation, daydreaming, and fantasizing. He enjoys projects which allow him to use his intuition and to express his feelings.

This type of learner needs to explore his creative abilities to find new ways to self-expression, to share his enthusiasm and his inspirations with others. He has an acute need to develop his own unique style of being. He has a keen interest in alternative belief systems, possibilities, and new projects. Things which may not have happened but may be made to happen are a source of continuing interest.

Most of all the Intuitive-Feeler is a learner who is at home with the multiple uses of metaphor, poetry, the forms language takes, and the visual and performing arts. NF's beliefs about what might be possible spur them on to find new solutions, to portray them artistically, and to do so with great enthusiasm. Their

creativity springs from within as they try to make peace between the outer problems of the world and their own inner need to be meaningfully involved in interpreting the world around them.

Thinking About Your Learning Style

The next phase of the self-assessment process is to look at yourself as a learner in terms of your strengths and needs for improvement.

The first part of this process is to analyze your responses from the **Learning Style Inventory** with your own subjective responses. Then, respond to the questions which follow as a way of putting the differences or distinctions into clearer focus.

Having now read the descriptions of the four learning styles and ranked them, compare your subjective responses with your responses to the **Learning Style Inventory**.

My Responses		L.S.I. Responses
_____	Dominant	_____
_____	Sub-Dominant	_____
_____	Tertiary	_____
_____	Inferior	_____

QUESTIONS TO CONSIDER:

1. What are your feelings about the results obtained up to this point about your style, e.g., are you comfortable, uncertain, pleased, confused? Why?

_____

_____

_____

_____

2. Are the characteristics of your style on target? Do they feel correct?

_____

_____

_____

_____

3. Do your subjective responses agree with your LSI profile? If not, where do you differ: dominant, sub-dominant, tertiary, or inferior?

_____

_____

_____

_____

4. What are some of the possible explanations for the lack of congruency between your subjective rankings and your LSI scores?

_____

_____

_____

_____

5. How does your dominant learning style compare with your personality type as identified in Chapter Four? Is it the same or different? What are some possible explanations for your personality type being different from your dominant learning style?

_____

_____

_____

_____

_____

6. What are the behaviors in your dominant learning style that you find most comfortable? Least comfortable? Why?

_____

_____

_____

_____

7. How is your dominant style an asset to you as a learner? How is it a liability?

_____

_____

_____

_____

8. How is your sub-dominant style an asset to you as a learner? How is it a liability?

_____

_____

_____

_____

9. How is your inferior or least developed style a liability?

_____

_____

_____

_____

10. Identify experiences when your inferior style was a liability?

_____

_____

_____

_____

11. What are some reasons for your reluctance to work in your inferior style?

_____

_____

_____

_____

12. What skills, by style, would you like to develop?

_____

_____

_____

_____

13. What are some of the things you could do to help expand your skills in this style?

_____

_____

_____

_____

14. What style do you rely on most in stressful situations? Is it your dominant?

_____

_____

_____

_____

15. What style (or styles) is (or are) most representative of how you function at your best? At your least competent?

_____

_____

_____

_____

16. What one style best characterizes your most academically successful students? Why do you believe this to be so? Is this same style your dominant style?

_____

_____

_____

_____

17. In what ways does your learning style influence your teaching behavior? List some specific examples.

_____

_____

_____

_____

Having completed these seventeen self-diagnostic questions, read the descriptions of learning abilities by styles. Identify those abilities you feel you would like to expand with a check (✔). Identify your strongest abilities with a plus sign (+).

ST ABILITIES	SF ABILITIES
— good at working with and remembering facts and details — able to speak and write directly to the point — approaches tasks in an organized and sequential manner — adapts to existing procedures and guidelines — concerned with utility and efficiency — goal oriented; focuses on immediate, tangible outcomes — knows what needs to be done and follows through — concerned with accuracy	— spontaneous and open to impulses, does what feels good — able to express personal feelings — aware of others' feelings and makes judgments based on personal likes and dislikes — learns through human interaction and personal experience — comfortable with activities requiring the expression of feelings — able to persuade people through personal interaction — keen observer of human nature — interested in people and acts on their behalf
NT ABILITIES	**NF ABILITIES**
— takes time to plan and contemplate consequences of actions — able to organize and synthesize information — weighs the evidence and risks judgment based on logic — learns vicariously through books and other symbolic forms — comfortable with activities requiring logical thinking — able to persuade people through logical analysis — retains and recalls large amounts of knowledge and information — interested in ideas, theories or concepts	— good at interpreting facts and details to see the broader picture — able to express ideas in new and unusual ways — approaches tasks in a variety of ways or in an exploratory manner — adapts to new situations and procedures quickly — concerned with beauty, symmetry and form — process oriented; interested in the future and solving problems of human welfare — concerned with creativity

On the basis of the strengths and needs you identified, which are your strongest and least-used styles? How do these styles match up with your own subjective analyses? How do these styles match up with the results of your **Learning Style Inventory**?

_____

_____

_____

_____

List below the learning abilities that you want to develop based on your own ranking

Learning Abilities I Need To Develop

_____

_____

_____

_____

_____

_____

_____

_____

_____

6

Understanding Myself As A Teacher

Introduction

Teacher self-assessment begins, as does any assessment process, in methodically collecting data about ourselves pertinent to our teaching roles and responsibilities. This process, like life itself, is ever changing! The motivation for undertaking such a journey is increased self-knowledge. The reward for this self-analysis is the making of better teaching decisions. The drive behind such self-analysis is the need and desire to become a more complete person and to hold out those same goals and aspirations for students.

As in Chapter Five, "Understanding Myself as a Learner," you will be given an opportunity to prepare for the self-analysis activities by working through some necessary warm-up activities, i.e., "My Ideal Teacher," and the "Self-Assessment Sentence Stem." These warm-up activities focus your attention on various teaching behaviors and preferences.

You will also have the opportunity of responding to the **Teaching Style Inventory**. The completion of the **Teaching Style Inventory** will assist you in the classification of your teaching behavior pertinent to ten different decision-making factors. They are:

1. classroom atmosphere
2. teaching techniques
3. planning
4. what one values in students
5. preferred working conditions
6. classroom management
7. preferred student behaviors
8. preferred teaching behaviors
9. student evaluation
10. teaching goals

The **Teaching Style Inventory**, similar to the **Learning Style Inventory**, is a self-descriptive diagnostic instrument based on Jung's theories of personality type. Also, as in the previous chapter, you will have an opportunity to compare your own perceptions of yourself as a teacher with the results of the **Teaching Style Inventory**.

Finally, we have included a series of questions to assist you in further analyzing your teaching style. Answering these questions provides a focus for ways to increase your teaching skills and/or ways to secure additional self-knowledge.

WARM-UP ACTIVITIES

Activity #1: Symbolic Representation of My Ideal Teacher
The following activity is designed to help you identify in symbolic form what you believe to be the ideal teacher.

Draw a symbolic representation, a picture or a stick figure, of your ideal teacher. The quality of your art work is not important. What is important is that you carefully consider the elements or characteristics you wish to include. Use symbols or words to describe your ideal teacher. Metaphors and similes are helpful in expressing ideas.

Once the drawing is completed, make a list of the words which describe the characteristics that apply to your drawing. Some of the characteristics may already be implicit in the design of the drawing while other characteristics may be implied. If you are working with a partner or are in a group situation, display the pictures on a wall and have a question-and-answer period. Look for similarities and differences.

SYMBOLIC REPRESENTATION OF MY IDEAL TEACHER

List the words that describe the characteristics of your ideal teacher.

_____

_____

_____

_____

Questions to Consider:

1. What do you value most about your ideal teacher?

_____

_____

_____

_____

2. What specific teacher behaviors, verbal and non-verbal, can you identify that reflect the characteristics of your ideal teacher?

_____

_____

_____

_____

3. What does your own teaching behavior look like compared to that of your ideal teacher? Is it similar? Different? Why?

_____

_____

_____

_____

Activity #2: Ten Things I Know About Myself as a Teacher:

Now let's take an introspective look. Reflect for a few minutes about your teaching behavior. The following questions may be helpful. These questions were not intended to be answered individually, but rather to act as a stimulus for thinking.

What kinds of behavior do I exhibit in my classroom?

What kinds of questions do I ask?

What kind of classroom environment do I try to establish?

What educational goals do I stress?

How do I deal with discipline?

How do I plan and manage instruction?

What kinds of things do I value in my students?

How do I see myself? How do others see me?

Under what conditions is it most enjoyable for me to teach?

What content areas do I most enjoy teaching?

What do I find most difficult about teaching?

What are the teaching techniques I use the most often?

What types of students do I most like to teach?

How do I manage my classes?

On the form which follows, fill in the perceptions and knowledge you have about yourself as a teacher. Begin each statement with "I." Be as specific and descriptive as you can.

TEN THINGS I KNOW ABOUT MYSELF AS A TEACHER

1. I _____

_____

2. I _____

_____

3. I _____

_____

4. I _____

_____

5. I _____

_____

6. I _____

_____

7. I _____

_____

8. I _____

_____

9. I _____

_____

10. I _____

_____

Next, analyze your statements by considering the following questions. As with your analysis of learning behaviors, you may wish to keep notes for later reference.

• What kind of classroom atmosphere or climate do I most prefer? Least prefer?

_____

_____

_____

_____

• What teaching techniques or strategies do I use most often? Least often?

_____

_____

_____

_____

• What role models do I emulate? Reject?

_____

_____

_____

_____

• What most satisfies me in my teaching? Makes me uncomfortable? Makes me angry?

_____

_____

_____

_____

• What works best for me in my teaching activities? What doesn't seem to work but should?

_____

_____

_____

_____

• What do I value most in my students? What least?

_____

_____

_____

_____

As you look at your responses consider these questions:

1. Which behaviors are reflective of your ideal teacher? Which are not? _____

_____

2. What areas of your teaching behavior give you the greatest satisfaction? How can you expand on these behaviors? _____

_____

3. What areas of your teaching behavior give you the least satisfaction? What immediate steps can you take to change these unsatisfactory behaviors? _____

_____

Activity #3: Self-Assessment Sentence Stems
This activity is designed to assist you in looking at your teaching behaviors against the variable or issues of planning, evaluation, goals, teaching techniques, etc. It should also help you identify satisfaction levels.

In completing the sentence stems below don't try to be too analytical. Generally, the first responses that come to mind are the most genuinely self-descriptive.

1. My classroom atmosphere emphasizes _____

_____

_____

2. My teaching techniques provide for _____

_____

_____

3. My teaching plans are _____

_____

_____

4. I like young people who _____

_____

_____

5. I am at my best when teaching students who _____

_____

_____

6. I manage my class by _____

_____

_____

7. As a teacher I tend to _____

_____

_____

8. I evaluate my students by _____

_____

_____

9. My students would describe me as _____

_____

_____

10. The most important goal of education is _____

_____

_____

11. My colleagues would describe me as _____

_____

_____

As you look back over each response, identify those you feel comfortable about, and those you'd like to change. Over the next several months repeat the activity and see how your responses change.

The Teaching Style Inventory

Now that you have focused on some of your values and teaching behaviors, a next step is to see how those same preferences are classified using the Teaching Style Inventory. The value of the Teaching Style Inventory can be expanded by responding to the items three different times as:

1. what you actually do as a result of your existing preferences.

2. what you would like to be able to do as next steps in improving your teaching skills.

3. what you think/feel are the ideal teacher behaviors.

As a procedure, we suggest you begin by thinking of a specific classroom situation (preferably a current one), and that you select responses based on how you actually function, i.e., what you really do now.

These initial responses now, and over time, may then be compared with your second and third sets of responses. At that point where the sets of responses tend to come into agreement with one another you will have changed your goals or your behaviors, or perhaps both. A first step is wanting to change. The second and more difficult step is practicing and mastering those skills necessary to change.

TEACHING STYLE INVENTORY

A self-diagnostic tool to identify one's teaching style profile

Developed by
Harvey F. Silver, Ed.D., J. Robert Hanson, Ed.D., & Richard W. Strong, M.A.
Revised October 1998

PURPOSE

The Teaching Style Inventory (T.S.I.) is a self-descriptive assessment of one's instructional decision-making. Based on the seminal research of C.G. Jung, the T.S.I. identifies a profile of teaching behaviors.

Directions:

Based on your analyses of seven decision-making categories, rank order the the descriptions that tend to best reflect the ways you make instructional decisions. Assign a 5 to the behavior that is the best measure of tendency; a 3 to the second; a 1 to the third; and a 0 to the least-used response.

As you read through the list of decision choices in each category, you may find it difficult to identify the response that best characterizes your general behavior.

This difficulty is understandable for a number of reasons: 1) we're often not aware of how we make decisions; 2) often the decision is made without an examination of alternatives; and 3) the context we teach in often dictates how we teach more than our own personal teaching style.

Such are the conditions of our humanness. In this instrument, however, our goal is self-insight through conscious reflection on how, most of the time, we tend to make our classroom decisions. The degree to which we can be bluntly truthful and forthright with ourselves is the degree to which the findings may be helpful in making us more aware of our decision-making processes. The aim of the instrument is to construct a profile for how we make decisions, not to evaluate our decision-making.

Please answer all questions. Make no ties. Generally your first response is the most self-reflective.

Silver Strong & Associates, Inc

The Thoughtful Education Press
1-800-962-4432

CHOOSING TEACHING PREFERENCES

In each of the following sets of behaviors, rank the four responses in order of:

First preference	5 Points
Second preference	3 Points
Third preference	1 Point
Fourth preference	No Points

Be sure to assign a different weighted number (5, 3, 1 or 0) to each of the four descriptors in the set. Do not make ties.

I. Planning

A. I am most comfortable when my plans are based on . . .

1. _____ key concepts and major themes
2. _____ established curriculum guides and test outlines
3. _____ the emotional and social needs of my students
4. _____ essential questions and project work

B. My plans frequently include . . .

5. _____ specific and well defined tasks
6. _____ a wide variety of materials, activities and projects with opportunities for students to make choices
7. _____ important issues to be analyzed and addressed
8. _____ activities intended to enhance self understanding, social interaction and group learning

II. Implementing

C. When applying my plans to the classroom I work hard to . . .

9. _____ follow my plans in an orderly and prescribed manner
10. _____ focus classroom interaction on essential questions and deep understandings
11. _____ connect my activities to my students' life experiences
12. _____ coach and stimulate my students to think divergently and be creative

III. Setting

D. The classroom atmosphere in which I am most comfortable emphasizes . . .

13. _____ interaction, collaboration, cooperation and comfortable conversation
14. _____ variety, stimulation, creative activity and project work
15. _____ intellectual challenge, serious inquiry and problem solving
16. _____ organization, clear tasks and purposeful activity to achieve mastery

E. I prefer my physical settings to be . . .

17. _____ a friendly, comfortable place for students to work in; that provides opportunities for students to sit in circles, to have conversations, and to work cooperatively.
18. _____ an inspiring and engaging place for students to work in; that has lots of interesting artifacts, is colorful, and has many resources for students to use and explore.
19. _____ an orderly, well-structured environment; a place for everything and everything has its place. A traditional setting where students are seated in rows or pairs and where efficiency is emphasized and the teacher is the primary focus.
20. _____ an intellectually stimulating room that promotes curiosity, debate and discussion; that has numerous books and resources for students to conduct independent study and extend their knowledge.

IV. Curriculum Objectives

F. In general, the major focus of the curriculum should be on . . .

21. _____ mastering skills and acquiring specific information
22. _____ developing a healthy self-concept and social skills
23. _____ interpreting and applying ideas and theories
24. _____ developing creative potential in all academic areas

V. Operations

G. The tasks I assign my students tend to focus on . . .

25. _____ workbooks, worksheets, recitation of information, practice exercises and programmed instruction
26. _____ essays, independent research projects, readings for meaning, investigations, debates and discussion of big ideas
27. _____ small group discussions, personal sharing, role playing, simulations, group projects, team games and other cooperative learning activities
28. _____ creative problem solving, long range projects, divergent expression, use of metaphor and artistic elements to express ideas

H. The work my students are required to do emphasizes . . .

29. _____ acquiring specific knowledge and skills; collecting, organizing and memorizing information
30. _____ understanding of big ideas; reasoning, analysis and problem solving
31. _____ self expression and synthesis of ideas; choice, craftsmanship and communication of ideas in new and original ways
32. _____ interpersonal connections and cooperation; describing one's feelings, working interdependently and personal reflection

VI. Roles

I. As a teacher I tend to play the role of . . .

33. _____ stimulator and facilitator
34. _____ intellectual challenger and content expert
35. _____ information giver, assigner of tasks
36. _____ nurturer and group facilitator

J. Strategies I frequently use include . . .

37. _____ creative production, non-traditional problem solving, metaphoric expression, creative writing and imaginative or inventive production
38. _____ debate, experiment, investigation and inquiry
39. _____ practice games, seatwork, short directive lectures, frequent exercises and repetition
40. _____ circle talks, students working as partners and group projects that emphasize helping ourselves and others

K. I enjoy it most when my students play the role of . . .

41. _____ problem solvers and researchers
42. _____ group members and community contributors
43. _____ innovators, resource finders
44. _____ hard workers and pragmatists

L. Qualities I most look for in my students include . . .

45. _____ logical analysis, pleasure in thought, a strong sense of pattern
46. _____ patience and tolerance with others, willingness to share feelings and work with others
47. _____ ingenuity, a sense of what's possible and aesthetics
48. _____ a sense of order, patience with clearly defined tasks, a willingness to work hard and take pride in achievement

VII. Evaluation

M. In evaluating students' learning I tend to rely heavily on . . .

49. _____ short answer exercises that ask students to reproduce work they have practiced in class
50. _____ essays, projects and problems that require the development of explanations, the use of evidence and the development of proofs
51. _____ day-to-day life in the classroom, personal qualities such as attention to detail, ability to concentrate, cooperation, paying attention
52. _____ projects and tasks requiring creative expression, imagination and the extension of learning to new contexts

N. In reviewing evaluation material I emphasize . . .

53. _____ what is measurable, quantifiable and accurate
54. _____ what is well thought out, soundly reasoned and interesting in formulation
55. _____ the amount of individual effort and student progress
56. _____ ingenuity, creativity, craftsmanship, the unusual and the unexpected

UNDERSTANDING DECISION-MAKING AS TEACHING BEHAVIORS

In each of the seven categories, the behaviors correspond to four different teaching styles. The teaching styles are based on the different ways people prefer to use their perception (sensing and intuition) and their judgment (thinking and feeling). The preference for either type of perception function is independent of the preference for either type of judgment function. As a result, four distinct combinations occur.

1) Sensing/Thinking (ST)   3) Intuitive/Thinking (NT)
2) Sensing/Feeling (SF)   4) Intuitive/Feeling (NF)

SCORING

I. SUBJECTIVE RANKING

Before scoring your Teaching Style Inventory please rank order the styles based upon your own immediate perceptions of your teaching preferences. Please carefully read the style descriptions which follow and then determine which description is most characteristic, next most characteristic, third most, and least characteristic. Remember that everyone operates in all four styles but that we tend to choose one particular style more often than the others.

Teaching Styles

Sensing/Thinking Teachers – are primarily outcomes-oriented (skills learned, projects completed). They maintain highly structured, well-organized classroom environments. Work is purposeful, emphasizing the acquisition of skills and information. Plans are clear and concise. Discipline is firm but fair. Teachers serve as the primary information source and give detailed directions for student learning.
(Preference _____)

Sensing/Feeling Teachers – are empathetic and people-oriented. Emphasis is placed on the students' personal life experiences and feelings of positive self-worth. The teacher shares personal feelings and experiences with students and attempts to build personal connections between and among students and the content they are learning. The teacher believes that school should be fun and introduces much learning through activities that involve the students actively and physically and allow for them to work cooperatively. Plans are changed frequently to meet the mood of the class or the feelings of the teacher.
(Preference _____)

Intuitive/Thinking Teachers – are intellectually-oriented. The teacher places primary importance on students' intellectual development. The teacher provides the time and the intellectual challenges to encourage students to develop skills in critical thinking, problem solving, logic, research techniques and independent study. Curriculum planning is developed around concepts frequently centering around a series of questions or themes. Evaluation is often based on open-ended questions, debates, essays or position papers.
(Preference _____)

Intuitive/Feeling Teachers – are innovation-oriented. The teacher encourages students to explore their creative abilities. Insights and innovative ideas are highly valued. Discussions revolve around generating possibilities and new relationships. The classroom environment is often full of creative clutter. The teacher encourages students to develop their own unique styles. Curriculum emphases focus on creative thinking, moral development, values, and flexible, imaginative approaches to learning. Curiosity, insight and artistic self-expression are welcomed.
(Preference _____)

Teaching Styles Profile

1. Most characteristic	3. Third most characteristic
2. Next most characteristic	4. Least characteristic

Scoring

To compute your score for each of the four decision-making areas, transfer your rank numbers from your answer sheet to the scoring sheet below. Compute your score by adding the rank numbers for each column.

	MASTERY ST	UNDER- STANDING NT	SELF- EXPRESSION NF	INTERPERSONAL/ SOCIAL SF
I. Planning				
A	2 _____	1 _____	4 _____	3 _____
B	5 _____	7 _____	6 _____	8 _____
II. Implementing				
C	9 _____	10 _____	12 _____	11 _____
III. Setting				
D	16 _____	15 _____	14 _____	13 _____
E	19 _____	20 _____	18 _____	17 _____
IV. Curriculum Objectives				
F	21 _____	23 _____	24 _____	22 _____
V. Operations				
G	25 _____	26 _____	28 _____	27 _____
H	29 _____	30 _____	31 _____	32 _____
VI. Roles				
I	35 _____	34 _____	33 _____	36 _____
J	39 _____	38 _____	37 _____	40 _____
K	44 _____	41 _____	43 _____	42 _____
L	48 _____	45 _____	47 _____	46 _____
VII. Evaluation				
M	49 _____	50 _____	52 _____	51 _____
N	53 _____	54 _____	56 _____	55 _____
TOTAL:	_____	_____	_____	_____

ANALYZING YOUR TEACHING PREFERENCES

STRENGTHS OF THE PREFERENCES

57 - 70	Very strong choice; very comfortable in the style
45 - 56	Strong choice; comfortable in the style
29 - 42	Moderate choice
15 - 28	Low comfort in the style
0 - 14	Very low comfort in the style

TEACHING PROFILE

No one teaching style adequately represents the complexity of one's teaching behavior. Everyone operates in a variety of ways in different situations. How demanding a particular learning challenge is, may determine how much one "flexes" or compensates by using other, often less preferred, styles. It's important, therefore, to identify not just one's dominant or most accessible style, but also one's entire profile. It is the full profile that gives the only accurate picture of how one functions. One's profile consists of four styles in a descending order of access. The dominant style is the most accessible because it is the most practiced. The auxiliary style is accessible with some additional effort. The third level (tertiary) and least developed (inferior) are such because they are not routinely practiced and therefore, are much less accessible. One's profile is always a hierarchy, but over time and with increasing consciousness, the tertiary and inferior functions can become more accessible as a result of practice.

MODE	SCORE	STYLE	COMFORT LEVEL	SUBJECTIVE RANKING (page 4)
Dominant				
Auxiliary				
Tertiary				
Inferior				

KNOWING YOUR SCORE*

A second way to interpret your scores is to go back and add up your subscores by **S**etting (items D and E); **C**urriculum objectives (item F); mental **O**perations (items G and H); **R**oles in class (items I, J, K, and L); and **E**valuation (items M and N). Enter the scores under the appropriate style heading. If you wish, color in the highest subscores for each of the five variables.

	MASTERY	UNDER-STANDING	SELF-EXPRESSION	INTERPERSONAL/ SOCIAL
S SETTING				
C CURRICULUM OBJECTIVES				
O OPERATION				
R ROLES				
E EVALUATION				

DIRECTIONS FOR PLOTTING YOUR TEACHING PROFILE:

Having completed the scoring of your teaching styles, plot your profile below. To plot your profile, mark the score you received for each style on the diagonal line that fits that style. Then connect your marks with a straight line to create a four-sided polygon. This configuration represents a visual presentation of your teaching profile.

VISUAL PRESENTATION OF MY TEACHING PROFILE

Sensing(s)

	ST	SF	
70			70
60		60	
45		45	
30		30	
15	15		

Thinking (T)

Feeling (F)

ST / NT

SF / NF

	15	15	
30		30	
45		45	
60		60	
70	NT	NF	70

Intuition (N)

QUESTIONS TO REFLECT UPON

The following questions will help you to reflect upon your results on the Teaching Style Inventory. Take a moment to review your analysis of the data, then respond to the following questions:

1. Which style is your dominant style? How is it an asset to you in your teaching? In what ways could your students benefit if you made greater use of this style in your teaching?

2. Which is your least used style? In what ways could your students benefit if you made greater use of this style in your teaching?

3. What should your students know about your teaching style and profile that would help them to be more successful in your class?

4. What changes would you like to make in your teaching profile? What knowledge, skills and attitudes would you need to further develop to make this change?

Learning Behaviors and Activities by Style

Interpersonal/ Social Sensing-Feelers	Mastery Sensing-Thinkers	Understanding Intuitive-Thinkers	Self-Expression Intuitive-Feelers
TEACHERS MAY BE CHARACTERIZED AS:			
Nurturers	Trainers	Intellectual challengers	Facilitators
Supporters	Information givers	Theoreticians	Stimulators
Empathizers	Instructional managers	Inquirers	Creators/Originators
LEARNERS MAY BE CHARACTERIZED AS:			
Sympathetic	Realistic	Logical	Curious
Friendly	Practical	Intellectual	Insightful
Interpersonal	Pragmatic	Knowledge oriented	Imaginative
CURRICULUM OBJECTIVES EMPHASIZE:			
Positive self-concept	Knowledge	Concept development	Creative expression
Socialization	Skills	Critical thinking	Moral development
SETTING (Learning Environments) EMPHASIZE:			
Personal warmth	Purposeful work	Discovery	Originality
Interaction/collaboration	Organization/competition	Inquiry/independence	Flexibility/imagination
OPERATIONS (Thinking and Feeling Processes) INCLUDE:			
Describing feelings	Observing	Classifying	Hypothesizing
Empathizing	Describing	Applying	Synthesizing
Responding	Memorizing	Comparing/contrasting	Metaphoric expression
Valuing	Translating	Analyzing	Divergent thinking
	Categorizing	Evaluating	Creating
TEACHING STRATEGIES INCLUDE:			
Circle	Command	Concept attainment	Synectics
Peer tutoring	Task	Inquiry	Moral dilemmas
Team Game Tournaments	Graduated difficulty	Concept formation	Divergent thinking
Group investigation	Programmed instruction	Expository teaching	Guided imagery
Role Playing	New American Lecture	Problem-solving	Metaphorical Problem-solving
STUDENT ACTIVITIES INCLUDE:			
Group projects	Work books	Independent study	Creative art activities
"Show and Tell"	Drill & Repetition	Essays	Imagining
Team Games	Demonstrations	Logic Problems	Boundary breaking
Directed art activities	Dioramas	Debates	Dramatics
Personal sharing	Competitions	Hypothesizing	Open-ended discussion
EVALUATION PROCEDURES INCLUDE:			
Personal journals	Objective tests	Open-ended questions	Fluency of expression
Sociograms	Checklists	Essays	Flexibility of response
Oral reports	Behavioral objectives	Demonstration of abilities to: apply	Originality of response
Ranking procedures	Use of mechanical devices	synthesize	Elaboration of detail
Trained observations	Demonstrations of specific skills	interpret	Development of aesthetic criteria
Collection of unobtrusive data	Criterion referenced tests	integrate	Producing creative products
Self-reporting	Normed tests	analyze	Artistic self-expression
	Teacher tests	evaluate	
		Aptitude for problem solving	

Characterizations of Teaching Styles

Having now completed an analysis of your teaching profile (your first, second, third, and last choices of styles), an opportunity is presented to rank order the four teaching styles based on detailed descriptions of each of the styles. These descriptions identify the recurring and most observable behaviors for each of the styles. By choosing a first, second, third, and last preference you have still more data for self-knowledge and the analysis of your teaching style.

As with learning styles, some precautionary notes are in order. First, the descriptions are inevitably stereotypic and general. No one teacher is precisely like the style described. Still, as a general picture the description identifies major behaviors and beliefs that may clarify the style for your own thinking. Second, teaching styles can only be described in terms of what is observable. Those observations always take place within a particular context or environment. Environments change and have an impact on behaviors. The descriptions, therefore, must be seen as generalizations without regard to context. Third, the teaching style used may not be the same as the teacher's personality type or learning style. Teachers must continually change their teaching styles to meet the needs of students and the objectives to be achieved. Fourth, no one style or profile is superior, in and of itself, to any other. Each style has its own strengths and weaknesses based upon context, content, and external pressures. What the descriptions or characterizations provide, therefore, is simply a sketch, an overview, of the dominant behaviors of each teaching style. Your own teaching style is discovered by filling in the sketch and by continually seeking to match your instructional intents with your observable behaviors.

The Sensing-Feeling Teacher

Overview
The Sensing-Feeling teacher is characterized by qualities of personal warmth, friendliness, empathy, concern for others and interpersonal relationships. She concentrates on the social and emotional adjustments of her students. She works in the "here and now" and often uses pupil interactions as the "content" for her teaching activities.

Approach To Teaching
The Sensing-Feeling teacher strives to establish a classroom atmosphere that supports student social interaction. She encourages her students to share their personal thoughts, feelings and experiences. She manages her classroom according to what "feels best." She may change a well-planned lesson on the spot if it does not feel right or if it is not responsive to the needs of her students. She believes that learning should and can be enjoyable because as the student learns and is confirmed in the learning he feels better. The Sensing-Feeling teacher also believes that school should be a place where students learn about themselves, develop constructive and rewarding relationships, and learn the necessary skills to get along and work cooperatively with others.

The Sensing-Feeling teacher wants to be liked by her students, peers, and significant others. She is sensitive to her students' personal needs both in and out of school. She enjoys personal contact with her students and outwardly expresses her affection for them.

The Sensing-Feeling teacher particularly values students who attempt to be honest with their feelings, are sensitive to the rights and feelings of others, and can work cooperatively.

The Sensing-Feeling teacher prefers to evaluate her students' achievement in light of the effort expended, individual abilities, personal problems and needs. She often relies on her own value judgments rather than on objective data. She is often influenced more by her own personal likes and dislikes than by external rules, procedures, or standards.

Issues of class conduct are handled by personal conferences and small group discussions. Class meetings are held as a way to establish socially acceptable behavior. Her approach to problems of discipline includes consideration of extenuating circumstances, her own appraisal of the personal significance of the infraction, and an attempt to understand the "intent" in contrast to the result of the infraction.

Her approach to teaching is one in which students can become personally involved in their learning. She tends to introduce new content by asking her students how they are personally related to the facts, ideas, objects, or places in question.

Commitment to learning is facilitated by demonstrating to the student his existing knowledge of what is being taught, i.e., the new content. Toward these ends she relies a great deal on discussions, group discovery projects, group awareness activities, exercises in clarifying communications, role-playing, acting out stories, participatory games in which no one loses, "show and tell," sharing personal feelings, and other kinds of interactive group process learning activities.

Assets and Liabilities

The Sensing-Feeling teacher is responsive to the social and emotional needs of her students. She recognizes each child as a person with his own unique potential. She develops a classroom atmosphere that is warm, friendly, and interactive. She encourages her students to value other peoples' feelings and to respect the rights of others. She attempts to utilize the experiences and interactions of her students to bring understanding to the content she is teaching. She helps her pupils understand and accept their feelings and to deal with their emotions more openly. Her classroom activities are creative mixtures of physical activity, i.e., active rather than passive learning, and they

focus on drama, service projects, discussions, and activities in which students are encouraged to express their feelings.

The Sensing-Feeling teacher's liabilities are that she may be overly involved in the personal problems of her pupils or peers. She may tend to overlook important content that has no feeling orientation. Science and math may end up short-changed in contrast to social studies, language arts, and history. She so needs to be appreciated that negative criticism or a lack of responsiveness from her students may sometimes be interpreted as a personal rejection. Her feelings are easily hurt. She may have an overly strong need for support and approval from those around her. She may also become easily discouraged or upset when things do not go as she had hoped. Her need to be liked or appreciated may thwart her ability to be objective, constructively critical, or firm in her decisions.

Teaches Best

The Sensing-Feeling teacher is at her best when teaching to her students' personal, social, and survival (coping) skills. She emphasizes process rather than product, i.e., how to work with people rather than for final results. She prefers to respond to the here-and-now rather than to the there-and-then, whether past or future. She capitalizes on spontaneous events for instructional insights.

She works best in cooperative situations with students and peers. She works best when content can be handled in small group instruction and interactions. She encourages peer tutoring. Her primary goals are reflected in activities providing for student feelings of self-worth, improved communication skills through self-expression, and the acquisition of social skills.

She teaches at her best when essential content can be directly related to pupils' experiences, when what students value is an overlay of some dimension of the content, and when pupils can make personal applications of the content.

Sensing-Feeling teachers are excellent models for finding ways to build to rapport and for seeing the ways to motivate pupils based on the commonalities of her student's experiences and the basic ideas of the required content.

The Sensing-Thinking Teacher

Overview

The Sensing-Thinking teacher is characterized by an orientation to hard work, efficiency, neatness, tasks, skills development, and the covering of the required content of the course or class. Her interests are with skills mastered and projects completed. Her emphasis is on product rather than process. She teaches in the here-and-now but makes continual reference to previously learned skills. She is pragmatic, realistic, and industrious. She plans her work and works her plan.

Approach To Teaching

The Sensing-Thinking teacher maintains a well-structured and highly organized classroom environment. There is a place for everything, and everything is in its place.

Students are encouraged to work in externally observable and purposeful ways: i.e., effort in and of itself is a value. There is a concentration on learning activities that are individually focused since the purpose of learning is skills mastery. Thus, her teaching techniques focus on drill, demonstration, competitions, recitations and workbook activities. The acquisition of information for its own sake is a value since learning is looked upon as work.

In class the Sensing-Thinking teacher spends most of her "talk time" giving directions and providing information. The information flow tends to be teacher-to-learner with students called on to provide the correct answers or to demonstrate the proper skills in response.

The Sensing-Thinking teacher's plans are clear and concise. She covers content in an orderly and prescribed manner, and generally does not vary appreciably from approved curricula.

The Sensing-Thinking teacher sets down, in advance, clearly defined classroom rules and procedures. She establishes clear expectations for student behavior. Such disciplinary procedures are usually in written form, e.g., class policies or rules or a class constitution. Student infractions of rules are met quickly, consistently, impersonally, and predictably. Sensing-Thinking teachers address discipline in a "firm but fair" manner.

Sensing-Thinking teachers value students who are task-oriented, well-organized, neat, respectful, prompt and prepared.

In evaluating her students' skill mastery, she makes extensive use of objective tests, quizzes, homework, recitation, and demonstrations. Her focus is on desired outcomes, i.e., on what is measurable, observable, testable, and justifiable. Classroom time is provided for students to demonstrate skills mastered or information learned.

The Sensing-Thinking teacher's instructional techniques make use of seat work, question-and-answer periods, practice, immediate responses to answers, worksheets, workbooks, hands-on activities, demonstrations, competitive games, lectures, audio-visual presentations, field trips, and craft projects.

Assets And Liabilities

The Sensing-Thinking teacher believes in hard work and the completion of required tasks. She is thorough and good at working with details. She covers all required course content within a classroom management system that is efficient and effective. She knows that required skills can only be learned by practice and repetition. She enjoys a full day of activities, in which everyone is involved and doing something. As students complete their work, she provides immediate feedback on its acceptability or correctness. She uses the energies that learners have in task-focused games. She reflects the outside world's concern for the acquisition of specific knowledge and skills. She rewards the hard workers and admonishes the slower students to achievement through greater effort. She is generally predictable, not easily flustered, and a reliable source of information. She assists students in learning self-discipline, competing for the best scores and grades, and learning the fundamentals for academic success. She tends to be methodical, concerned with clarity in providing instructions, and businesslike in establishing the learning environment.

The liabilities of the Sensing-Thinking teacher are that she may overlook the individual learner's needs in the push for content or skills mastery. She may overemphasize detail to the point where the students become bored or discouraged. Her concern with rules may make her appear rigid or unfeeling. The concern for order and organization may result in such regimentation that students get "turned off." Her dependency on lesson plans and fixed curriculum guides may mean that she overlooks the spontaneous instructional content of the classroom. Her over reliance on pat procedures may make it difficult for her to adapt to an ever-changing classroom environment. She may tend to become set in her ways.

As the primary information giver, she may discourage students from searching for answers from other sources. Her thrust toward convergent teaching strategies may distract students from looking for other alternatives. As the giver of directions, she may end up suppressing any natural leadership tendencies on the part of students.

Teaches Best
The Sensing-Thinking teacher is at her best when instructing in skills mastery or information recall through drill and repetition. She teaches best from well-defined objectives and specific resource materials. She excels in teaching those content areas that are linear and cumulative. Organization, planning, outlining,

cataloging, rule-making, and planning procedures are second nature for her. She teaches best where students can see the practicality and utility of what's expected. For students who need or want immediate responses to their work she is pleased to comply.

The Sensing-Thinking teacher is less comfortable working in open-ended, interactive situations without well-defined objectives, rules, resources, or procedures. She tends not to choose work of a hypothetical or abstract nature. She wants and needs to know what the end results of her labors are to be. She has identical expectations for her students.

The Intuitive-Thinking Teacher

Overview
The Intuitive-Thinking teacher is characterized by an orientation to ideas, theories, concepts, and rational thought. She emphasizes the ability to think critically and independently. She emphasizes the need to discover and apply knowledge to solving problems and thinking in terms of cause and effect. Her goal is to develop her students' intellectual abilities. She seeks knowledge and understanding.

Approach To Teaching
The Intuitive-Thinking teacher's approach to teaching emphasizes the posing of intellectual questions, making available extensive resources and materials, and providing for learning through discovery. Lessons are designed to be intellectually stimulating; to emphasize the development of critical thinking skills; and to present students with opportunities to deduce consequences, to compare and contrast, to analyze, to synthesize, and to evaluate. Her instructional strategies rely heavily on wide-based reading, the attainment of concepts, divergent thinking, games of strategy, debate, open-ended questioning, problem-solving, brainstorming, and independent study projects that have a research orientation. Her verbal teaching behaviors make extensive use of the Socratic method in which the student, through questions and answers, discovers truth within

his own experience. She lectures frequently, makes extensive use of existing theory, and constantly asks her students to hypothesize about relationships. The hypotheses, hers or her students', become the basis for the assignment of independent study projects.

The Intuitive-Thinking teacher appreciates students who demonstrate intellectual maturity for their age group, can make defensible analyses, are excited by ideas, can handle symbol systems (language, math, logic, etc.) and can work well independently.

The Intuitive-Thinking teacher prefers to manage her classroom and questions of discipline by having open discussions on the need for rules, seeking responses to what might happen if there were no rules or authorities, and having the class prepare their own conventions for acceptable behavior. Classroom problems are presented to the students as issues to be analyzed and worked through. School rules that are not defensible in terms of reasoning or logic tend to be overlooked. She looks for good judgment and common sense on the part of her students and is sometimes annoyed by her students' immature behavior.

The Intuitive-Thinking teacher's teaching behavior emphasizes the acquisition of knowledge and the development of intelligence. She serves as resource person to her students and assists them in their personal intellectual inquiries. Her verbal behaviors stress the search

for causes, hence, she constantly asks, "Why," "What are the reasons," and "What would happen if…?"

In evaluating her students' performance, she is more concerned about their understanding the general idea, principle or formula than about precise, detailed answers. As a result she makes extensive use of essay questions, open-ended test questions, research projects, knowledge of pertinent resources, the writing of position papers, debates, and demonstrations of the students' mastery and integration of concepts and rules.

Assets And Liabilities

The Intuitive-Thinking teacher's assets are in presenting ideas and concepts. She brings enthusiasm and commitment to the teaching of the great ideas and to assisting students in learning to think critically and independently. She is a superb organizer of resource materials and can stimulate high levels of student involvement in discussing controversial questions. She is expert at turning problem situations into opportunities for problem-solving by looking dispassionately at causes and their probable effects. She has a unique ability for translating ideas into learning experiences appropriate to the age group of her class. She encourages an open attitude of exploration— both to assist the pupil in learning what is within himself, as well as to incorporate the knowledge of the larger world outside himself. She provides an atmosphere of challenging opportunities, innovativeness, and learner independence.

The Intuitive-Thinking teacher's liabilities are often reflected in an absence of commitment to pertinent detail. She may overlook the need for the mastery of certain basic skills in students who speak well and think logically.

In providing a stimulating learning atmosphere, she may fail to specify precisely what is to be learned, or completely frustrate the learner who needs detailed instruction. Her concern about teaching ideas may baffle the student who needs to be addressed in the "here and now" and her disposition to independent study projects may genuinely frustrate those students who need to work in small groups or tutorial relationships.

Her emphasis on cognitive growth may be to the detriment of how pupils may be feeling. The open-endedness of her questions may frustrate those sensing students that need to have limits set.

In her relationships with her peers, she may appear aloof or overly intellectual. Her apparent lack of concern over school rules may frustrate central office personnel. On school committees she may frustrate other members by being more concerned about doing something conceptually sound than by trying out something and staying on schedule.

The Intuitive-Thinking teacher may tend to speak over the heads of her students, to be too critical (especially for the Sensing-Feeling student), and to withhold praise or approval when it is really called for.

Teaches Best

The Intuitive-Thinking teacher is at her best when presenting broad concepts and themes. She is uncomfortable when required to follow a predetermined "who," "what" and "when" outline.

She teaches best when the desired learning comes from student responses to ideas and theories, and when her students can secure pertinent detail on their own. She works best when questioning students and leading them to their own conclusions rather than telling them what the answers are or precisely how to arrive at solutions. She works best in developing her own goals and objectives rather than being responsible for predigested materials. She teaches best when she has a wide array of materials and resources and can peruse her students' interests in making her points rather than being confined to workbooks, practices, or drills.

The Intuitive-Feeling Teacher

Overview

The Intuitive-Feeling teacher is characterized as enthusiastic, insightful, and innovative. She tends to be a creative and an aesthetically motivated person. She tries to inspire her students to explore possibilities and to find ways to better express themselves. Innovation and creativity are highly valued. The Intuitive-Feeling teacher's students generally discover that they have gifts and talents of which they were previously unaware.

The Intuitive-Feeling teacher tends to be morally sensitive and alert. She has a keen sense of her own personal beliefs. She tends to be a practitioners of one or more of the arts. She pays particular attention to beauty, symmetry, harmony, and the aesthetic qualities of things or ideas.

Approaches To Teaching

The Intuitive-Feeling teacher emphasizes the abilities and processes involved in thinking creatively, imaginatively, and aesthetically. She places a heavy premium on assisting students in exploring the inner world of possibilities.

In her classroom she provides for a flexible, innovative atmosphere with myriad resources to stimulate the learner's creative and thinking abilities. There are few restrictions in her classroom. To the passer-by the room seems like a place of chaotic yet purposeful work. A major objective is to stimulate the learner's curiosity.

The Intuitive-Feeling teacher most appreciates those students who have original insights and ideas, who are concerned with the larger issues of justice and morality, who question the way things are done, and who can express themselves in creative and artistic ways.

The Intuitive-Feeling teacher arranges her class day so that students are challenged and so that these challenges can be responded to in a flexible way. In providing learning experiences for her students, she concentrates more on the richness and personal investedness of the student than in specific measurable outcomes. The purpose of these enrichment activities is to assist students in feeling and thinking through the consequences of their knowledge and behavior in order to help them think more clearly about who they are, as well as what they wish to become. The Intuitive-Feeling teacher assists her students in looking for their individual and unique potentials and in expressing those potentials in creative ways.

The Intuitive-Feeling teacher's teaching behavior tends to be marked by spurts of insight, a high energy level, a tolerance or confusion
and clutter, and an openness to alternative means of expression. She is also very concerned about her students as persons, and relates to them as co-searcher and friend rather than as an authority figure.

In evaluating her students, the Intuitive-Feeling teacher is very aware of the personal circumstances surrounding each student's work. She brings high levels of empathy to bear in assessing student outcomes and evaluates those outcomes in light of the student's own needs. A student's creative work is judged for its artistic merit, its theme and subject matter, and the degree to which it represents the learner's maturity and aesthetic sense. Intuitive-Feeling teachers are committed to assisting students in becoming increasingly self-reliant, articulate, and independent.

Assets And Liabilities

The Intuitive-Feeling teacher's assets include the ability to stimulate curiosity, to challenge the imagination, and to think about values in personal terms. She can empathize and establish close personal relationships with students and peers. She is a fountain of good ideas and is open to the ideas of others. She elicits responses from her students as a preferred way of communicating content. She is typically enthusiastic because she can relate what she is doing in class to her own and her students' values. Her acute interpersonal perception and judgment make her alert to what is happening in the class and to using class situations as learning experiences. She is a role model for solving problems openly and creatively.

On the other hand, her liabilities may be that her creative approach to learning sometimes leaves unexamined the need for detailed planning and for the identification of required resources for ambitious tasks. Her need to improve things may sometimes result in routine chores being overlooked or underdeveloped. Intuitive-Feeling teachers may put off paperwork until it reaches a crisis level. Students who need continual reinforcement in learning the basics may feel they have been offered too much too soon when they are still grasping after the specifics of what is to be learned. By the same token, there may sometimes be confusion over precisely what it is that students are required to learn since so much time and energy is committed to getting a broader, global picture of life and its values. In other words, her liabilities may suggest that she is more interested in the future than the present. She may overlook the need to rehearse students in the basic skills and be disappointed when the students need extensive individual instruction or can't seem to relate to the intellectual and creative challenges of the classroom. Her concern with the larger issues of justice and morality may be too abstract for some of the more sensing-based learners. She may become so involved in the non-directive approaches to learning that students become confused about precisely what it is they are to learn or what they are to be held accountable for. She may become so involved with the articulate and creative students that she ignores or overlooks those struggling to keep up. Students who have difficulty in sharing their feelings, talking about their goals, or becoming involved in service projects may not get the time they need to develop their own skills and value systems. Her enthusiasm may be seen by some as an effort to impose her own values on her students and peers. Her peers sometimes see her as impulsive, subjective and somewhat unpredictable. She is disappointed when her class does not match her enthusiasm and commitment to a task.

Teaches Best

The Intuitive-Feeling teacher is at her best when stimulating her students to respond creatively to problem situations. She is most effective when establishing rich learning experiences based on personal trust. The exploration of new possibilities and unusual or creative solutions to pupil-identified problems is a favored area for discussion. She is frustrated by classroom work requiring extensive drill, memorization, and repetition.

She is at her best when identifying resource materials and working environments that result in pupil interactions on social issues. She is most comfortable as an orchestrator of dramatic productions, role-plays, artistic exhibits, and debates on social issues. She is less comfortable in the areas of discipline or requirements that her classroom be traditionally organized. She is at her best in making the learning situation exciting, creative, stimulating, and personally relevant to her students.

She is at her best when classroom activities can be channeled to address student needs and interests. She works best with students who have strong personal interests and who demonstrate concern over aesthetic and moral issues. Her educational goals focus on assisting students in clarifying their own unique potential, and describing those beliefs in imaginative and artistic ways. Her classroom is a chaotic clutter of animated learners, rich in resources and meaningful human relationships. She works to develop student competencies, creative abilities, and interpersonal skills founded on well-articulated moral thought and discussion.

Thinking About Your Teaching Style

The next phase of the self-assessment process is to look at yourself as a teacher in terms of your strengths and needs for improvement.

The first part of this process is to analyze your responses from the **Teaching Style Inventory** with your subjective responses; then, to respond to the questions which follow as a way to put the differences or distinctions into clearer relief.

As with the ranking of your learning styles in Chapter Five, you are encouraged to rank and then to compare your subjective responses with your responses to the **Teaching Style Inventory**.

My Responses		T.S.I. Responses
_____	Dominant	_____
_____	Sub-Dominant	_____
_____	Tertiary	_____
_____	Inferior	_____

Analyzing your teaching styles and preferences requires the same careful reflection as did the consideration of your learning styles. A step in the direction of conducting such an analysis is the thoughtful completion of the questions which follow.

1. Do your subjective responses agree with your **Teaching Style Inventory** profile? If not, where do the differences occur?

_____

_____

_____

_____

_____

_____

2. If there are disagreements, what might some of the possible explanations be?

_____

_____

_____

_____

_____

_____

3. How does your teaching style profile compare with your learning style profile? Are they the same? If not, on what levels are they different, i.e., dominant, sub-dominant, tertiary or inferior? What are some of the possible reasons for the difference?

_____

_____

_____

_____

_____

_____

4. List at least two examples of your teaching behavior that represent your dominant style or superior functions.

_____

_____

_____

_____

_____

5. In what ways has your dominant style served as an asset in the classroom? Give two or three examples.

_____

_____

_____

_____

_____

_____

6. In what ways has your dominant style served as a liability in the classroom? With what kinds of students? Give examples. Think of students who could have been better served if you had used other teaching styles.

_____

_____

_____

_____

_____

_____

7. List two examples of times when a lack of skills in your inferior style led to problems in your classroom.

_____

_____

_____

_____

_____

_____

8. What styles(s) were you using when answering questions 6 and 7?

_____

_____

_____

_____

_____

_____

Having completed these eight self-diagnostic questions, read the descriptions of teacher abilities by styles. Identify those abilities in which you feel you need improvement with a check (✔). Identify your strongest abilities with a plus sign (+).

Sensing-Feeling Teaching Abilities

__establishes a warm, friendly, supportive atmosphere in which students are encouraged to interact with one another, work cooperatively, and share their personal thoughts, feelings, and experiences.

__comfortable with shifting from prescribed plans in order to respond to the here-and-now class needs and moods; capitalizes on spontaneous events for instruction.

__encourages students to be involved personally and emotionally in their learning.

__adept at working with students who are sensitive, need to be nurtured, and prefer to work interactively and collaboratively with others.

__establishes appropriate student behavior by developing positive relationships with students, face-to-face communications, and small group meetings.

__encourages students to be honest with their feelings, sensitive to the rights and feelings of others, and work cooperatively.

__comfortable with interactive and collaborative teaching techniques emphasizing fun, student interactions, and personal experiences as content.

__evaluates student achievement in light of effort made, ability, need, and personal problems.

Intuitive-Thinking Teaching Abilities

__establishes an intellectually stimulating atmosphere in which students are provided with a variety of resources and activities designed to challenge their thinking abilities, develop their analytical skills, and stretch their limits of performance.

__comfortable planning in broad outlines around key open-ended questions or themes in which main concepts or ideas are identified and looked at from several directions and disciplines.

__encourages students to think for themselves, to discover and apply knowledge and concepts to new problems.

__adept at working with students who are mature and knowledgeable, excited by ideas, and prefer research projects and independent work assignments.

__establishes appropriate student behavior by helping students to examine the basis of and justification for rules.

__encourages students to think for themselves, to ask why, to use their reasoning skills, to be logical, and to strive for perfection.

__comfortable with teaching strategies that encourage critical thinking emphasizing planning, independent research projects, inductive and deductive reasoning, and problem-solving techniques.

__evaluates students' ability to reason and apply what has been learned through the use of open-ended questions, real life problems, and through their demonstration of abilities to apply, analyze, synthesize, and evaluate ideas.

Sensing-Thinking Teaching Abilities

__establishes an organized, systematic, activity-oriented, teacher-directed atmosphere in which students are engaged in purposeful work.

__able to follow prescribed guides or texts which are translated into weekly or daily plans.

__adept at working with students who are competitive, action-oriented, and who learn best from direct experience and step-by-step procedures.

__establishes well-defined rules and procedures for covering content in an orderly and prescribed manner.

__establishes appropriate behavior by setting clear standards and expectations set for students.

__encourages students to be goal-oriented, to apply themselves to the task at hand, to be neat, organized, and punctual, and to follow rules and procedures.

__utilizes programmed instruction, behavioral objectives, demonstrations, and teacher-directed activities to help students acquire mastery of specific content and skills.

__evaluates student skills using precise behavioral measures (true or false tests), observations, student demonstrations, frequent tests or quizzes, and criterion referenced measures.

Intuitive-Feeling Teaching Abilities

__establishes a flexible, innovative atmosphere with a minimum of restrictions in which students are encouraged to express their creative abilities and to design their own activities for learning.

__able to use curriculum guides, texts, and materials as resources for a constantly changing curriculum based on the interests and curiosities of the students.

__adept at working with students who have strong personal interests, insights original ideas and who question the way things are done.

__utilizes open-ended discussions, moral dilemmas, creative and artistic activities to enable students to explore their creative abilities, to find ways of self-expression, to gain inspiration, and to explore personal values.

__evaluates student skills by judging creativity, flexibility, fluency, and originality of responses; uses observations, peer juries, personal aesthetic criteria and creative artistic products.

__establishes appropriate behavior by assisting students to think/feel through the consequences and the significance of their actions in order to enable them to acquire an internal sense of discipline.

__encourages students to look for new ways of doing things, to follow their inspirations, to be open to the unusual, and not to be confined by convention.

On the basis of the strengths and needs you identified, which are your strongest and least used styles? How do these styles match up with your own subjective analyses? Your **Learning Style Inventory** results? Your **Teaching Style Inventory** results?

List below the teaching abilities that you want to develop based on your own ranking.

Teaching Abilities I Need to Develop
As a final step in the identification of your teaching behaviors, answer the questions which follow.

FOLLOW-UP QUESTIONS TO ANSWER:

1. How might I use all four styles in my classroom? In my school committee work? In my goals for personal and professional growth?

_____

_____

_____

_____

_____

_____

2. How does my preferred teaching style affect the unsuccessful students in my class?

_____

_____

_____

_____

_____

_____

3. How does my preferred teaching style affect the gifted and talented students in my class? The artists? The dreamers?

_____

_____

_____

_____

_____

_____

4. What do I want my students to know about me in terms of my learning and teaching preferences?

_____

_____

_____

_____

_____

_____

5. How can I share my insights about my students' learning styles with their parents?

_____

_____

_____

_____

_____

6. How are my teaching and learning styles reflected in my curriculum planning? Management? My evaluation of students? My classroom?

_____

_____

_____

_____

_____

7. How can I share my most personal insights and goals with my peers? My supervisors?

_____

_____

_____

_____

_____

8. How can I teach the Thoughtful Education model to my students?

_____

_____

_____

_____

_____

9. Do my responses to these questions alter my rankings or selections of teaching abilities? How?

_____

_____

_____

_____

_____

Writing Personal Goals

The responses you make to these questions, along with the data from the tests and exercises, constitute the conduct of a subjective personal and professional self-assessment. A next step is to think through this new information, to rank your findings in terms of greatest needs perceived, and then to set a few short- and long-range goals for yourself.

The proposed short-term goals must be things that you can definitely accomplish within a week or a month. It is important that these short-term goals are personally meaningful to you and that they are, in fact, doable. Experiencing success with these short-term goals will contribute to the setting of the more difficult long-term goals.

A key to bringing about desired changes in your teaching behavior is to actually write down what you want to do, how well you want to do it, and by what date you plan to accomplish it. This written record may be revised as needed. The point is that you have committed yourself to professional and personal growth goals. The key to behavioral change is action. As with the learning of a skill, mastery only comes with practice. You cannot read about it. You must risk doing it. Thinking about changing simply will not provide the results you want.

Examples of short-term goals might be to spend 20 minutes a day planning and teaching in your tertiary or inferior styles, or to identify a student who learns differently from you and to plan a lesson with him over required content in his preferred learning style.

Writing Personal Short-Term Goals to Improve Your Teaching

Some suggested first steps:

1. Review your findings from the previous exercises and tests. What are the areas of greatest need that you identified that you would like to change? What does this desired change mean in terms of specific short-term behaviors?

2. List as many, or as few, of these behaviors as are really important to you for your personal and professional growth.

Examples:

___to be able to ask questions and assign tasks in the Intuitive-Thinking mode

___to be able to set up a warm, reinforcing atmosphere for the discussion of personal values

___to identify alternative ways of reinforcing basic skills in math, etc.

3. Rank these needs statements on the basis of most important to least important.

4. Select the top two (or three) and brainstorm or otherwise determine how to do some specific new behaviors in response to these needs.

Examples:

___Learn how to use games in reinforcing basic skills and memory work. Identify said games.

___Identify and read a book on questioning techniques in the Intuitive-Thinking domain.

___Identify, read about and practice problem-solving activities in small groups.

___Identify resource people who can assist me in designing creative arts projects and materials for my social studies unit.

5. Now select one specific action from the above that you can successfully complete in a week or ten days.

6. Convert that action into a measurably stated objective by writing **What** you will do, **How Well** you will do it, and by **When**.

Examples:

___By next Friday afternoon, I will have read one book on problem-solving, and will have engaged six students in actually solving a class problem of importance to them.

___By the end of the month, I will have identified two basic skills reinforcement games, have tried them both out in class on that week's spelling words, and have selected the one game that seems best for class use based on increased scores and students' opinions on learning the required words.

1. My greatest needs

_____
_____
_____
_____
_____
_____
_____
_____
_____

2. My needs in the rank order of their importance to me

_____
_____
_____
_____
_____
_____
_____

3. Possible responses to these needs: short term, doable activities

_____
_____
_____
_____
_____
_____
_____

4. My objectives (what, how well, and by when)

_____
_____
_____
_____
_____
_____
_____

7

Understanding Learning Styles And Profiles

Introduction

No person is just a single learning style! Such a belief would only lead to another labeling system. Rather, Jung's Analytic Psychology leads the hungry learner to the more comprehensive and satisfying conclusion that the complex makeup of the human psyche means everyone is all the styles and both of the attitudes. Yes, one style and one attitude do dominate because they were the most affirmed in one's early years, and because affirmed by those we loved have been the most practiced. One's dominant style becomes that upon which one depends. One's dominant style works! It's how we got through school. It's how we succeed on the job… or don't. But in any event one's dominant style is one's dependency. And because it has worked well for us we've left the other functions and attitude undeveloped because unpracticed.

Yet all the things we aspire to do, or to have our students do, remain but dreams. Our psyches are telling us through these wishes that we have these undeveloped capacities and that they must be exercised. Jung reminds us that the psyche is a self-regulating organ. Like the heart, kidneys or lungs, conscious behavior does not direct their functioning. We don't tell the heart when to beat or the lungs when to exhale. Similarly, the psyche controls consciousness. One of the psyche's demands, like the lung's demand for oxygen, is that we be whole, individual, self-activating and psychologically healthy. In other words, our own biological makeup will not allow us to develop only one style or one attitude to the exclusion of the others.

The energy to make the changes that we've always wanted to make reside in the exercise of the lesser or undeveloped functions. A paradox of our human existence is that our dominant style is our greatest weakness! Why? Because by so depending on our dominant style we've neglected the other styles that represent our greatest potential strengths! The learner's profile then gives us the only picture upon which teachers can diagnose *and* prescribe to all the needs of the learner.

The challenge of teaching is twofold: First, to be aware of one's own profile, one's strengths and weaknesses, and, second, to know one's students as profiles with their strengths and weaknesses. To teach to the whole child means to teach to the learner's profile; to affirm these in their dominant style, and to support and challenge them in the development of their lesser styles.

Collecting Learning Profile Information

There are several methods for uncovering a learner's profile. Some of this information we have already, e.g., subjects in which the student excels, activities the student enjoys, books the student reads (or doesn't), memberships the student finds satisfying, etc. These are all examples of data collection that in the aggregate says something about the student based on observation and the collection of unobtrusive data. Categorizing these interests as style dependencies provides the focus necessary.

A second form of data collection is through direct interview. Utilizing the thoughtful education model and varying the way one asks questions across the four styles reveals a kind of verbally based style profile.

A third method would be direct observation over time, again, utilizing the model as a way of categorizing satisfying versus unsatisfying activities. With 30 students, or with 150 students, direct observation is often not practical. Sometimes others, e.g., paraprofessionals or parents, can be trained to do this kind of observation, but at best the process is either cumbersome or expensive.

A fourth choice is the use of instrumentation. Self-reporting instruments are quick, inexpensive and practical ways to get a lot of information. The drawbacks to any self-report instrumentation is the student's degree of self-awareness and the ability (difficult for us all) to make distinctions between what we are and what we think we ought to be. In most cases instrumentation is almost a necessity since the other systems are time and money dependent. In short, if we don't test we don't get the information we need.

In any event profile information must be collected and interpreted based on some theoretical construct of psyche or mind. The thoughtful education model uses an instrument based on Jung's type behaviors. The *Hanson-Silver Learning Preference Inventory* is a 144 item forced choice instrument that provides data on style dependencies and attitude. Each item has a stem phrase followed by four choices which the respondent puts in a 1-2-3-4 order with "1" representing the most favored choice.

There are many style assessment instruments. All the instruments necessarily reflect a theoretical model. It is the model's comprehensiveness that determines the instrument's utility. At the present time (1996) there is only one instrument for school-based populations that uses Jung's concepts of type and psychic structure, and that has a specifically instructional focus. That instrument is The *Learning Preference Inventory*. Please see Appendix A for a description of other style models: Appendix B for the statistical analysis of the LPI, and Appendix C for a sample LPI printout.

When teachers administer The Learning Preference Inventory they receive a printout on each student (see sample in Appendix C) that graphically depicts the student's profile, i.e., the scores for each of the four styles, plus scores for introversion and extroversion.

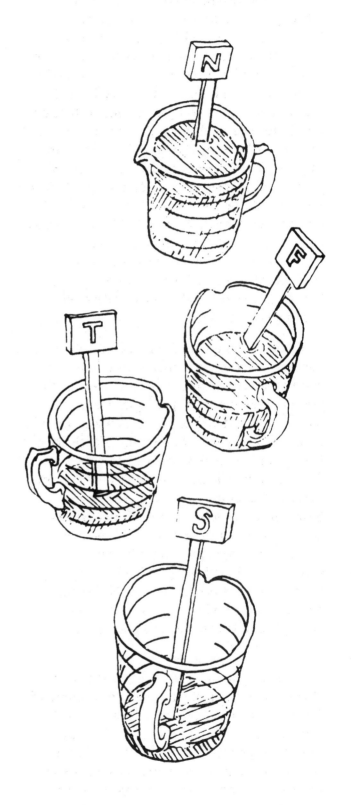

Hanson Silver

LEARNING PREFERENCE INVENTORY

A classroom diagnosis tool
for teaching, learning and curriculum planning.

Developed by
Harvey F. Silver and J. Robert Hanson
Revised 1991

STUDENT NAME

FIRST NAME	LAST NAME	MI

(Bubble grid with letters A–Z for each name column)

DATE			AGE	GRADE	SEX	ETHNIC GROUP	STUDENT IDENTIFICATION NUMBER
Month	Day	Year					

SEX: Male / Female

ETHNIC GROUP:
- American Indian
- Asian
- Pacific Islander
- Filipino
- Hispanic
- Black
- White
- Other

(Numeric bubble grids 0–9 for Date, Age, Grade, and Student Identification Number)

PLEASE DO NOT MAKE ANY STRAY MARKS IN THIS SHADED AREA

109899

INTRODUCTION

Knowing more about how one learns makes schooling more enjoyable and the learning experience more effective. Information from Hanson-Silver Learning Preference Inventory helps you and your teachers make better decisions about learning and teaching.

The Learning Preference Inventory is not a test. There are no right or wrong answers. There is no time limit. And, it is not a reading test. So, if you're having trouble with a word or phrase, please ask your teacher for help.

DIRECTIONS FOR RESPONDING

The Learning Preference Inventory (LPI) is made up of 36 statements followed by four choices with four circles in front of each choice numbered 1-4. For each of the statements rank order for four choices. Fill in the circle in the choice for your first choice with the 1 bubble, mark only one circle in each choice. Continue on till you have made 4 choices. See Example:

1. I prefer learning something new by

①	②	●	④	reading a book	(Third Choice)
●	②	③	④	watching a movie	(First Choice)
①	②	③	●	making a project	(Fourth Choice)
①	●	③	④	working with a friend	(Second Choice)

The most important thing to remember is to rank each answer according to how you feel, not how you think you ought to feel. Make your own choices based on your best judgment.

---

1. I'm good at
- ① ② ③ ④ helping others
- ① ② ③ ④ getting things done
- ① ② ③ ④ organizing things
- ① ② ③ ④ discovering things

2. I like questions that ask me
- ① ② ③ ④ to think of new and original ideas
- ① ② ③ ④ to explain why things happen
- ① ② ③ ④ to choose the correct answer
- ① ② ③ ④ how I feel about things

3. In a group I am usually
- ① ② ③ ④ quiet
- ① ② ③ ④ noisy
- ① ② ③ ④ talkative
- ① ② ③ ④ listening

4. When I'm making something I prefer to
- ① ② ③ ④ have someone show me how to do it
- ① ② ③ ④ follow the directions one step at a time
- ① ② ③ ④ figure out how to do it by myself
- ① ② ③ ④ find a new way for doing it

5. I would like to be in
- ① ② ③ ④ music, painting or writing
- ① ② ③ ④ science, math or law
- ① ② ③ ④ business, politics or construction
- ① ② ③ ④ sales, social work or nursing

6. As a person I tend to
- ① ② ③ ④ be hard to get to know
- ① ② ③ ④ talk easily about my feelings and ideas
- ① ② ③ ④ be easy to get to know
- ① ② ③ ④ keep my thoughts and feelings to myself

7. I work best when
- ① ② ③ ④ I'm having fun
- ① ② ③ ④ I know exactly what I have to do
- ① ② ③ ④ I'm finding a solution to a problem
- ① ② ③ ④ I can choose what I want to learn

8. I like assignments or activities which involve
- ① ② ③ ④ taking ideas and changing them into something new and different
- ① ② ③ ④ searching for solutions to problems
- ① ② ③ ④ copying or making things
- ① ② ③ ④ sharing my feelings and ideas

9. When I'm working I tend to
- ① ② ③ ④ be careful
- ① ② ③ ④ do things quickly
- ① ② ③ ④ be impatient with work that takes a long time
- ① ② ③ ④ work with something that takes a long time

GO ON TO NEXT PAGE

THANK YOU FOR NOT MAKING STRAY MARKS IN THIS AREA

10. **When I have a difficult assignment I like to**
    ① ② ③ ④ talk with others to see what needs to be done
    ① ② ③ ④ memorize or practice what needs to be done
    ① ② ③ ④ think things through for myself before someone explains it to me
    ① ② ③ ④ find new or different ways of doing the assignment

11. **I enjoy**
    ① ② ③ ④ doing things I've never done before
    ① ② ③ ④ reading about things that interest me
    ① ② ③ ④ doing things I know about and can do well
    ① ② ③ ④ working with friends

12. **I like**
    ① ② ③ ④ quiet places where I can think
    ① ② ③ ④ noisy and crowded places where lots of things are happening
    ① ② ③ ④ doing lots of different things at the same time
    ① ② ③ ④ doing one thing at a time

13. **I prefer games that**
    ① ② ③ ④ everyone can play and where no one loses
    ① ② ③ ④ are fast, have a lot of action, and where someone wins
    ① ② ③ ④ make me think ahead about what to do (Chess, Stratego, etc.)
    ① ② ③ ④ require me to use my imagination

14. **I would like to**
    ① ② ③ ④ create art, music or dance
    ① ② ③ ④ invent or discover something
    ① ② ③ ④ make a lot of money
    ① ② ③ ④ help other people

15. **When working on an assignment I prefer working**
    ① ② ③ ④ in a quiet place
    ① ② ③ ④ in a group with other people
    ① ② ③ ④ in a place where I can talk and share with other people
    ① ② ③ ④ by myself

16. **People who know me well would say I'm mostly**
    ① ② ③ ④ caring, friendly and helpful
    ① ② ③ ④ neat, fast and accurate
    ① ② ③ ④ logical, sensible and intelligent
    ① ② ③ ④ creative, enthusiastic and imaginative

17. **In school the most important thing to me is**
    ① ② ③ ④ using my ideas and imagination
    ① ② ③ ④ learning how to think and reason for myself
    ① ② ③ ④ getting good grades
    ① ② ③ ④ making friends

18. **When I meet new people I**
    ① ② ③ ④ find it difficult to think of good things to say
    ① ② ③ ④ feel comfortable and talk easily
    ① ② ③ ④ enjoy talking about myself
    ① ② ③ ④ feel uncomfortable talking with people I don't know

19. **I like to learn about**
    ① ② ③ ④ myself and other people
    ① ② ③ ④ things I can do and use
    ① ② ③ ④ important ideas and why things happen
    ① ② ③ ④ what life may be like in the future

20. **I would like a job where I can**
    ① ② ③ ④ make and do unusual things
    ① ② ③ ④ read and think
    ① ② ③ ④ make useful things
    ① ② ③ ④ work with people

21. **When I feel upset I**
    ① ② ③ ④ have difficulty telling others how I really feel
    ① ② ③ ④ share my feelings easily
    ① ② ③ ④ usually let everybody know how I feel
    ① ② ③ ④ keep my feelings to myself

22. **When I have a problem I like to**
    ① ② ③ ④ work with a partner
    ① ② ③ ④ work it out step by step
    ① ② ③ ④ think about it and then make a plan
    ① ② ③ ④ find a new way to solve it

23. **When I have many assignments to do I**
    ① ② ③ ④ want to move on to something else once I've learned how to do it
    ① ② ③ ④ think carefully about what needs to be done, and then plan how best to do it
    ① ② ③ ④ start working right away and finish one assignment before beginning another
    ① ② ③ ④ take time to talk with others and check my answers while I work

GO ON TO NEXT PAGE ➡

THANK YOU FOR NOT MAKING STRAY MARKS IN THIS AREA

24. In group activities I
① ② ③ ④ listen to what others have to say before I speak
① ② ③ ④ share my own ideas first and then get reactions
① ② ③ ④ talk a great deal
① ② ③ ④ keep my ideas to myself until I'm asked to speak

25. I like books about
① ② ③ ④ people's feelings and personal problems
① ② ③ ④ real people (biographies), adventure stories, and how to make things
① ② ③ ④ mysteries, science, and stories that explain why things happen
① ② ③ ④ legends, fantasies, and other people's beliefs

26. I like assignments that
① ② ③ ④ are new and different
① ② ③ ④ make me think
① ② ③ ④ I know and can do well
① ② ③ ④ have people working together helping each other

27. I really enjoy
① ② ③ ④ reading and thinking
① ② ③ ④ being with people
① ② ③ ④ talking
① ② ③ ④ writing

28. I am at my best when
① ② ③ ④ working in a group
① ② ③ ④ knowing exactly what to do
① ② ③ ④ finding information and thinking
① ② ③ ④ making up my own ideas

29. I like to
① ② ③ ④ use my imagination
① ② ③ ④ investigate ideas
① ② ③ ④ make something that I can use
① ② ③ ④ hear what other people have to say about themselves or about me

30. When I'm working I prefer to
① ② ③ ④ think a lot before starting
① ② ③ ④ start right away and think about what I'm doing as I go along
① ② ③ ④ do many things at the same time
① ② ③ ④ do one thing carefully before beginning the next

31. My best ideas come from
① ② ③ ④ talking with people
① ② ③ ④ doing things
① ② ③ ④ reading about things
① ② ③ ④ imagining things

32. I prefer teachers who
① ② ③ ④ encourage me to be creative
① ② ③ ④ make me think
① ② ③ ④ teach me how to do useful things
① ② ③ ④ want to be my friend

33. I prefer assignments that
① ② ③ ④ have people working to help each other
① ② ③ ④ I can do quickly and well
① ② ③ ④ make me think, and may take a long time
① ② ③ ④ allow me to express my feelings and use my imagination

34. I prefer to learn by
① ② ③ ④ doing an original project
① ② ③ ④ reading and discovering things for myself
① ② ③ ④ answering questions in a workbook or on worksheets
① ② ③ ④ playing a game

35. I learn best when I can
① ② ③ ④ share my ideas with others
① ② ③ ④ apply skills I've already learned or memorized
① ② ③ ④ look things up and compare ideas
① ② ③ ④ do projects of my own choosing

36. Answering these questions was
① ② ③ ④ fun
① ② ③ ④ frustrating
① ② ③ ④ difficult
① ② ③ ④ easy

THANK YOU FOR COMPLETING THIS INVENTORY
PLEASE ERASE ANY STRAY PENCIL MARKS ON THIS FORM

PLEASE DO NOT MAKE ANY STRAY MARKS IN THIS SHADED AREA

109899

Interpreting a Student's Profile

The *Hanson-Silver Learning Preference Inventory* (HSLPI) provides profile data on students, ages 8 and up, indicating dominant, sub-dominant, tertiary and inferior (undeveloped and therefore inaccessible) sets of functions. This graphic portrayal (see Profile 1) of the learner's capacities provides the teacher with a rich set of alternatives for working more effectively with both assets and liabilities. In effect there are eight (8) sets of dominant styles, i.e., introverted/ extraverted modifying the ST, NT, SF, and NF styles.

The graphic profile (see Profile 1) signals the relative strength of each of the student's four sets of styles, and of the dominant attitude (I/E). Style dominances are the respondent's recognition of those most highly used functions. Each style is a measure of a dependency and, hence, a central tendency.

This same student needs, after having been validated in the dominant style, to be challenged to function more effectively in the inferior function. To work with intuitive capacity, the student must practice, in short time-frames and with frequent and positive teacher feedback the skills of imagination, imaging (seeing specific pictures in their minds), responding to their hunches about things, using metaphor to look at things differently, hearing/reading stories about intuitive characters, e.g., how inventors, discoverers, etc. really did or found something, seeing connections, looking for underlying patterns and rules, learning to withhold judgment and suspend disbelief, and learning to look for other alternatives and possibilities. The skills of intuition manifest themselves in academic work in their conclusions rather than in their processes, i.e., if a student makes an insightful inference, or draws an articulate conclusion, the student is commended for his or her thinking! But the thinking was only made possible because of the student's intuitive capacity. The admonition for teachers is that if they want the latter, they must teach the student the former! Textbook and convergent factually-based testing emphasizes sensation to the virtual exclusion of intuition. It is intuition, however, on the higher levels of schooling that is essential to academic success.

The profile also indicates the most highly developed single function. In the case of the following profile, the dominant function is sensation (S) because it received the two highest sets of scores. Intuitive (N) capacity is the more undeveloped, and therefore, inaccessible. A teacher responding to this profile would validate the learner by arranging for academically successful experiences based on a heavy concentration of sensing-based learning activities, e.g., use of manipulatives, worksheets, frequent true/false quizzes, whole-body involvement, use of music, rhythm, tastes, different sounds, workbooks, tools, competitive exercises, peer-partnerships, lots of opportunities to talk and ask questions, frequent and positive feedback and both teacher and student demonstrations of skills.

Our student's profile also indicates a strong preference for extraversion. In a nutshell this means this student learns best and will retain the most if the required content is processed verbally. The extravert functions best when required content is processed in dyads and small groups, at frequent intervals, during the class. Extraverts learn by thinking out loud, by trying things out verbally, and by hearing what other people think. Vocabulary development is accelerated among extraverts as they hear themselves using, in context, the new words. Homework works best for extraverts when they first see it modeled and explained, they practice and explain it to one another, and then go home to complete it.

A second and opposite profile, (see Profile 2), displays a learner who is highly intuitive and introverted.

This profile dramatizes acute introversion, i.e., this student strongly prefers to work alone, dislikes dyads or small group discussions, probably requires quiet and some isolation for doing his or her best work, dislikes being hurried, and tends to remain silent during class.

PROFILE 1

Learning Profile Report for:

age: 15   grade: 9   ethnic group:
Student number: 15122

Dominant Learning Styles:

Sensing-Thinking   73
Sensing-Feeling   48

Least used Learning Styles:

Intuitive-Feeling   29
Intuitive-Thinking   29

Quadrant Graph:

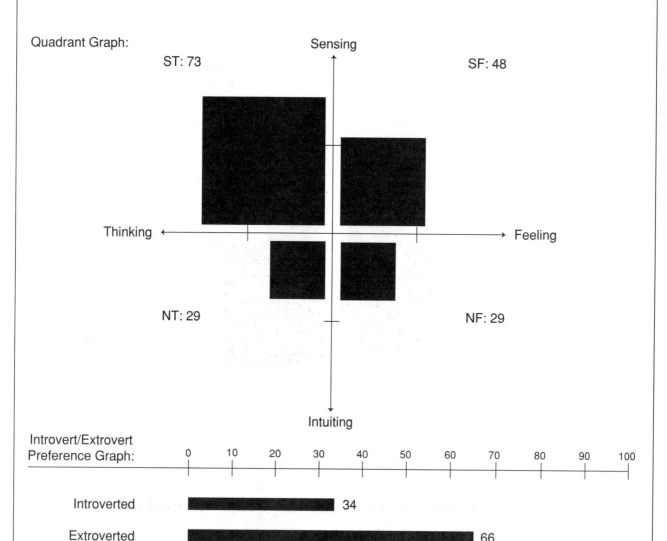

Introvert/Extrovert
Preference Graph:

Introverted   34

Extroverted   66

Notes:

1) The four learning styles scores are each independent measures.
   Therefore, the style scores should not be expected to total 100.

2) Improperly marked items are not scored.
   On this survey all of the 36 questions were properly marked.

PROFILE 2

Learning Profile Report for:

age: 14   grade: 9   ethnic group:
Student number: 15128

Dominant Learning Styles:

Intuitive-Feeling   70
Intuitive-Thinking   57

Least used Learning Styles:

Sensing-Feeling   31
Sensing-Thinking   22

Quadrant Graph:

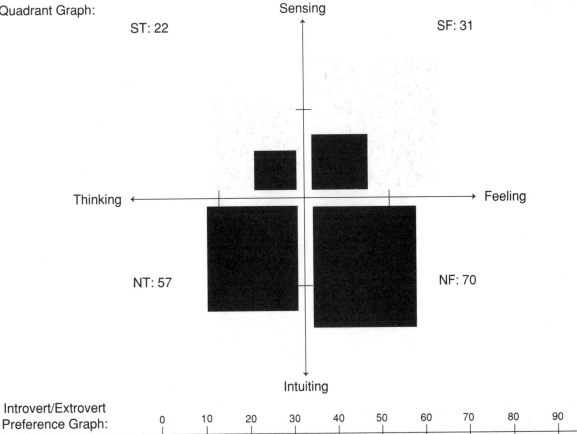

ST: 22   Sensing   SF: 31

Thinking   Feeling

NT: 57   NF: 70

Intuiting

Introvert/Extrovert
Preference Graph:

0   10   20   30   40   50   60   70   80   90   100

Introverted   80

Extroverted   20

Notes:

1) The four learning styles scores are each independent measures.
   Therefore, the style scores should not be expected to total 100.

2) Improperly marked items are not scored.
   On this survey 35 of the 36 questions were properly marked.

The key issue to remember in working with introverts is their need for processing time. Overall, introverts tend to fare better academically than do their extraverted peers. The introvert processes information more intensely than the extravert because the introvert must relate what's being learned to what they, personally, value and to how it fits with their prior experience. They have a need to let things "stew." These processes take time. Introverts are not slow learners; rather, they are deep learners. Once the strong introvert has reached a conclusion they usually have an eloquent defense. The fore-warned teacher who wants to validate strong introverts needs to organize dyads and discussion groups such that the introvert can prepare in advance. Penalizing strong introverts for not participating in discussion groups without advance warning is counterproductive for both teacher and student.

Our second student's highly developed intuitive capacity suggests the ability to do high-level academic work. Intuitive capacity in both the thinking and feeling domains suggests two critical keys to academic success; for the thinking dimension high vocabulary development, and for the affective dimension, high imaginative and creative capacity. In the lower grades this profile must compensate out-of-style to be successful. In the upper grades the verbal analytic, imaginistic and creative capacities serve the student well for those tasks requiring inference, induction, aesthetic appreciation and original thought.

A third profile (see Profile 3) illustrates a highly developed extraverted feeler… to the virtual exclusion of the thinking and introverted operations. This is the profile of a student who will have difficulty in most of his/her academic experience. Highly developed feelers drop out of school in the single largest numbers (69% of a normal distribution of at-risk learners), and also are the teacher's biggest challenge since their preferred modes of learning are through talk and the expression of feeling.

In this third profile the teacher's challenge on the feeling side is to build experiences in the required content that specifically relate to the learner's experiences. Building "bridges" between the required content and the student's own life experience addresses the feeler's questions about relevance, motivation, capacity to learn, and the related affective issues about anxiety and learning, e.g., "can I really do this?"

This profile reveals a student who probably has lots of friends, talks easily, is physically very involved in student activities, thinks creatively, is artistic and/or very imaginative, is a good story-teller, probably doesn't enjoy reading, is very dramatic, dresses non-traditionally, has occasionally brilliant insights into human behavior, has a strong social and moral sense, and struggles, painfully, for self-understanding in a school world he or she sees essentially as impersonal if not overtly hostile.

The teacher's challenge is to hook this student's interest by arranging for the expression of feelings, discussions about the relevance of content to the student's life experience, arranging for lots of resources and art/music materials so students can demonstrate thinking applications, design class so that students work can be exhibited, teach visual acuity skills, invite non-written responses to course content, e.g., art, drama, role-plays, mime, music, poetry, choral work, photography, sculpture and sand-play, etc. To work effectively with feeling-dominant learners is to work more effectively with all students!

Portfolios, authentic assessment tasks, logs, and journals are nearly perfect process and product measurement systems for the SF/NF learners.

Finally, the fourth profile (see Profile 4) is that of a dominantly thinking and balanced attitudinal type. This profile shows a slight tendency toward extraversion, but not enough to inhibit independent thinking capacity or to hinder homework. Independent seat work would require only modest compensations.

PROFILE 3

Learning Profile Report for:

age: 14   grade: 9   ethnic group:

Student number: 15124

Dominant Learning Styles:

Sensing-Feeling   72

Intuitive-Feeling   66

Least used Learning Styles:

Sensing-Thinking   22

Intuitive-Thinking   20

Quadrant Graph:

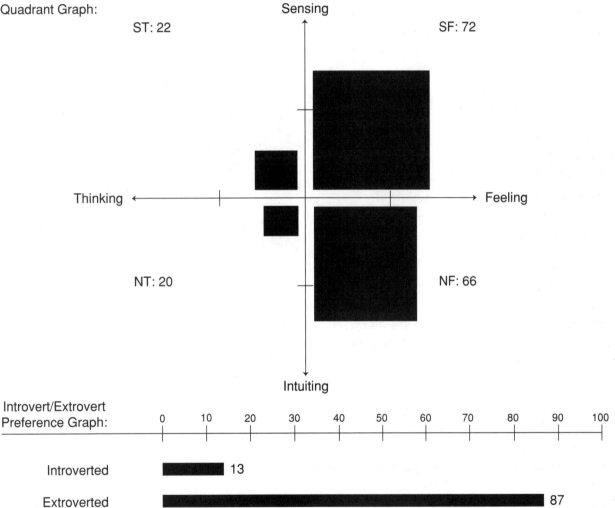

ST: 22

Sensing

SF: 72

Thinking

Feeling

NT: 20

NF: 66

Intuiting

Introvert/Extrovert
Preference Graph:

0   10   20   30   40   50   60   70   80   90   100

Introverted   13

Extroverted   87

Notes:

1) The four learning styles scores are each independent measures.
   Therefore, the style scores should not be expected to total 100.

2) Improperly marked items are not scored.
   On this survey 35 of the 36 questions were properly marked.

PROFILE 4

Learning Profile Report for:

age: 14   grade: 9   ethnic group:
Student number: 15347

Dominant Learning Styles:

Intuitive-Thinking   56
Sensing-Thinking   54

Least used Learning Styles:

Sensing-Feeling   46
Intuitive-Feeling   25

Quadrant Graph:

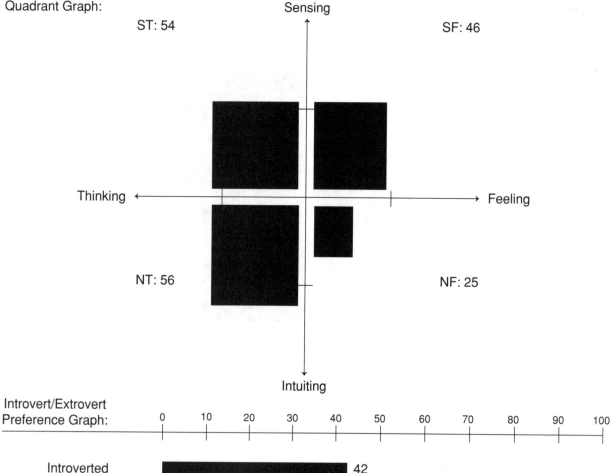

Introvert/Extrovert
Preference Graph:

Introverted 42

Extroverted 58

Notes:

1) The four learning styles scores are each independent measures.
   Therefore, the style scores should not be expected to total 100.

2) Improperly marked items are not scored.
   On this survey 35 of the 36 questions were properly marked.

This student's dominant thinking orientation suggests s/he will do well, academically, on both the lower and upper levels of school. The capacity to work in both the sensing and intuitive modes reveals a lower school capacity to organize, to remember, to exercise self-discipline, and to think convergently. On the upper school levels the intuitive capacity to infer, induce, conceptualize, analyze, and process divergently suggests few compensatory behaviors will be required to be academically successful.

The teacher's challenge with this profile will be to affirm the student's thinking capacities while simultaneously developing the feeling functions. Generally this is an awesome task since academically successful thinking-types usually don't have much recognition of affective need and/or believe feelings have little to do with school. In this regard the teacher will want, little by little, to introduce the strong feelers to the skills of empathy, coaching others who need assistance, leadership skills, active listening skills, appreciation of other learning profiles and learning how to identify, acknowledge and express their own feelings.

An Observational Procedure: Checklist of Preferred Behaviors

Sometimes a teacher knows immediately, if not intuitively, that a student's LPI scores and profile are not right. The reasons are multiple, e.g., the student is responding as s/he thinks s/he should; or as s/he thinks is correct.

When the teacher is in doubt on one or two students, a possible solution is to observe those youngsters over a five to ten day period using the checklist which follows. Generally, within a few days, a pattern will emerge.

The best of all possible ways to get an accurate reading on those students in question is to deliberately rotate instruction around each of the style dominances, and to make one's observations at those crucial points.

Hanson Silver Strong & Associates, Inc.

The TLC
LEARNING PREFERENCE INVENTORY

A classroom diagnostic tool
for teaching, learning and curriculum planning

Developed by
Dr. Harvey F. Silver and J. Robert Hanson

CHECKLIST OF PREFERRED BEHAVIORS

(A learning styles assessment tool prepared by Hanson Silver Strong and Associates, Princeton Junction, NJ)

Pupil's Name _____ Date _____

School _____ Grade _____ Age _____

Teacher or person completing this form _____

How long have you known this student? _____

Hanson Silver Strong & Associates, Inc.
34 Washington Road, Princeton Junction, NJ 08550

ST Behavior Descriptors (Sensing-Thinking)

1. _____ Is interested in things that are practical and that have immediate use.
2. _____ Speaks and writes directly to the point.
3. _____ Needs to be active, to be engaged in concrete exploration and hands-on manipulation, rather than working with abstract ideas or theories.
4. _____ Prefers assignments which require right or wrong responses rather than open-ended interpretations.
5. _____ Approaches tasks and chores in the classroom in an organized, efficient, systematic manner; cleans up thoroughly and efficiently; pushes all the chairs under the table; likes to see an ordered classroom.
6. _____ Prefers practicing skills already mastered (overlearning) rather than attempting to learn new ones (e.g., would rather show you he/she can count to 20 than learn to count by two's to 20).
7. _____ Learns best by doing things with the hands or by engaging directly in activities.
8. _____ May ignore or not be aware of other people's feelings.
9. _____ Likes an established routine and is impatient with complicated procedures.
10. _____ Likes to repeat and share factual information with the class to show how much he/she knows that others don't know.
11. _____ Likes graphs and records of his/her accomplishments noted with stars, stickers, etc. on a class chart for all to see.
12. _____ Wants needs met and problems solved immediately; prefers not to have to figure things out for himself/herself; doesn't like to wait; is often impatient.
13. _____ Enjoys competition, learning games, and will work for grades or gold stars, etc.
14. _____ Likes the schedule for the day printed on the board and reviewed at the start of the day.
15. _____ Needs to know what is expected of him/her, what is to be done, how it should be done, what the final product will look like, and when it is to be completed.

Total _____

SF Behavior Descriptors (Sensing-Feeling)

1. _____ Is warm, friendly, sociable, open, outgoing.
2. _____ Is spontaneous and sometimes impulsive; may put his/her "foot in mouth" after reacting with an immediate impulse, rather than thinking first.
3. _____ Allows personal choices and preferences to be influenced by peers; looks around the room to see how others are voting or signaling before making a decision.
4. _____ Works well with peers in a group; likes to play the role of "helper."
5. _____ Would rather discuss things that directly affect people's lives (accidents, moving to a new town, everyday happenings, sports) or things that have direct connections to his/her own life or to the community.
6. _____ Is interested in classmates and speaks out for or acts on their behalf.
7. _____ Shows little interest in impersonal facts, theories, headline news, politics, government, geography, etc. unless it can be directly related to personal experience or someone he/she knows and cares about.
8. _____ Prefers to learn by means of stories; makes personal connections to stories.
9. _____ Prefers to do things he/she knows and can do well rather than to try something new.
10. _____ Enjoys messy activities which allow for the expression of feelings.
11. _____ Enjoys chatting with others, sometimes to the point of ignoring classwork.
12. _____ Stories are usually lengthy and detailed; finds it difficult to be brief, concise, to the point.
13. _____ Has feelings easily hurt or cries when constructive suggestions and criticism are given; has to talk about feelings and responses in such situations.
14. _____ Needs frequent praise and encouragement to attempt new learning or to complete difficult work.
15. _____ Prefers a warm, friendly classroom environment where he/she can relax, move about, feel comfortable and "at home."

Total _____

Style

Highest Score	Dominant
Second Highest Score	Sub-Dominant
Third Highest Score	Tertiary
Lowest Score	Inferior

Directions
Rate the behaviors for each style using the following scale.
Rating Scale
1 = seldom or never
2 = occasionally
3 = usually

NT Behavior Descriptors (Intuitive-Thinking)

1. _____ Is good at explaining things, connecting ideas which are not clear, and making reasonable conclusions. Enjoys asking why and explaining why.
2. _____ Is good at reasoning things out for him/herself; doesn't wait around for others to do it.
3. _____ Is comfortable with ideas, current events, and other "adult" topics.
4. _____ Enjoys multiple-step tasks that are challenging and can't be done quickly or easily.
5. _____ Usually thinks things through before speaking; does not speak off the top of his/her head; thinks first, listens to others, analyzes what's been said, then adds a unique, logical perspective.
6. _____ Likes to discuss headlines, news stories, big ideas, the effects of these ideas on the world at large.
7. _____ Takes time to plan and think things through before beginning to work on an assignment.
8. _____ Argues a point on logic, reason, factual information, not on emotion, feelings, whim or preferences.
9. _____ Is good at games of strategy where it is necessary to anticipate several moves in advance.
10. _____ Demonstrates ease with spoken and written language, expresses self clearly, logically and in detail; summarizes and evaluates well.
11. _____ Sets high standards for himself/herself and others; gets anxious and "down on himself/herself" if those standards aren't met or errors are made; can be judgmental of others if they don't meet the standards he/she has preset for them.
12. _____ Organizes ideas; structures things, people, situations, ideas, information; is often a class leader who delegates and helps others get things done.
13. _____ May ignore or not understand the "feeling" or emotional responses of other children.
14. _____ Learns mainly through reading; does not need to personally experience something or to manipulate items in order to understand it.
15. _____ Prefers a bookish, problem-based classroom which encourages thinking, explaining, and debating ideas.
Total _____

NF Behavior Descriptors (Intuitive-Feeling)

1. _____ Is comfortable using his/her imagination, making up games and stories with "crazy connections," and engaging in creative, dramatic play.
2. _____ Is interested in alternatives, possibilities, new projects, and things which have not happened but may be made to happen.
3. _____ Will go to great lengths to create work or stories that are unlike anything else produced in the class; sees self as an "artist," "writer," or "musician."
4. _____ Expresses himself/herself in unique, unusual ways; stories may be larger than life or exaggerations of what actually happened.
5. _____ Speaks with emphasis, drama, facial expression, gestures and body movements; has a personal style or certain "pizzazz" or "flair."
6. _____ Has fun with things that aren't reasonable and may seem silly to most; enjoys thinking about "what if" questions.
7. _____ Is able to improvise and to adapt quickly to new situations and procedures.
8. _____ Is sensitive to beauty and symmetry, and will attend to the aesthetic characteristics of things.
9. _____ Does not conform to other students' ideas or behavior; has his/her own unique style.
10. _____ Is interested in the future, what might be, and what could happen.
11. _____ Does not like to be told what to do or how to do it; prefers doing things his/her way in his/her own time frame; choice is paramount; marches to own drum.
12. _____ Uses similes and metaphors; often personifies inanimate objects; comfortable in presenting ideas with pictures, icons, or symbolic images.
13. _____ Engages in many projects at once, sometimes completing none of them; can handle multiple projects but not deadlines.
14. _____ Gets the "gist" or the big picture; looks beyond facts and details to "see the forest"; sees a broader perspective.
15. _____ Can be spontaneous and open to change and the unusual; is not "hemmed in" by routines, "should be's," or the way things are ordinarily done.
Total _____

ANALYZING THE STRENGTHS OF THE PREFERENCES

STRENGTHS OF THE PREFERENCES

STRENGTHS	STYLE SCORE	ATTITUDE SCORE
Very high preference	100-125	64-80
High preference	75-99	48-63
Moderate preference	50-74	32-47
Some preference	25-49	16-31
Little or no preference	0-24	0-15

DIRECTIONS FOR PLOTTING STUDENT PROFILES

Having completed the score of the student's preferences, plot the student's profile below. To plot the profile, enter the scores by style in the spaces provided from the highest score (dominant) to the lowest (least used). Then enter a point or dot in the appropriate column for each score. Finally, connect the points with straight lines. This plotting provides a visual estimate of the relative strengths of each style.

LEARNING PREFERENCE INVENTORY PROFILE

PREFERENCE	STYLE	SCORE	PLOT					
			0	25	50	75	100	125
Dominant								
Sub-Dominant								
Tertiary								
Inferior								

ATTITUDE PROFILE

ATTITUDE	SCORE	PLOT					
		0	16	32	48	64	80
Extraversion							
Introversion							

Finally, you may wish to transfer your own perceptions from the Checklist of Preferred Student Behaviors to the chart below for comparison with the scores and strengths from the Learning Preference Inventory.

BEHAVIOR CHECKLIST PROFILE

Of Student Learning Preferences from the checklist of Preferred Student Behaviors.

Preference	Style
Dominant	
Sub-Dominant	
Tertiary	
Inferior	

Please refer to the User's Manual for more detailed suggestions on interpreting and making use of the Learning Preference Inventory.

Conclusions

Everyone's profile illustrates assets and liabilities. Everyone has both. Assets suggest skills that have been assimilated through years of practice. In the latter, the student needs to be affirmed. In the former, the student needs to be supported and challenged. Essentially the two valances (assets versus liabilities) can be interpreted as opposite sides of the same capacity, just as coins have heads and tails, and electrical charges are both positive and negative.

The learning profile is proof positive of the polarized or oppositional nature of our human make-up, e.g., everyone is both weak and strong, slow and insightful, loving and apathetic, nurturing and aggressive, etc. So with the profile teachers get a "picture" of both the outer and inner child, the negative film exposed revealing, in reverse, a positive print.

At this point you've self-assessed as a learner and as a teacher. Then in Chapter Seven you were introduced to a style instrument, and to a supportive behavioral check list. Now, you're ready to look at some of the decisions you can make based on the collected data.

8

Using The Learning Style/ Profile Model: Deciding What To Do

Styles, Strengths and Disabilities

Introduction

The previously described learning (and teaching) model is a comprehensive tool for interpreting and integrating all the dimensions of learning. Its applications cover all the cognitive, affective, perceptual, emotional and conscious dimensions of any learning task. As such, the model is a map of how the mind operates. As a map, the model points to all the possible ways there are to think about things and come to conclusions, but the model, as a map of possibilities, doesn't indicate direction. Teachers, as "travelers," must both know where they want to go, and how to read the map to be successful in promoting learning for all students across all content.

This learning model is complex. Like engineers studying percolation rates in different soils, the water passes through some soils more rapidly than others. Similarly, readers need to give themselves permission to learn and integrate these ideas and skills at their own pace. And as with any skills, competence can only come with application, practice, self-assessment, and more practice.

The purpose of this model is to demonstrate the processes involved in self-realization in the context of learning required school content on simultaneously deeper and broader levels. By challenging the learner to learn any set of ideas or skills across all the styles the teacher has also led students in the processes of self-discovery. These two emphases are inseparable. If students are to be able to learn at their maximum capacity, they must first be engaged on the level of personal feelings. Affect is the door to motivation and involvement. The student's feelings about what is to be learned either accelerate or retard their cognitive capacities. Therefore, to engage the students' psyches we must first focus on the student as a self. The self as having unlimited potential, but also the self as being comprised of both developed and undeveloped capacities.

Having invited students' recognition of their psyches in the process of acknowledging their feelings, we must also challenge their cognitive capacities. Serendipitously, as we teach any content across all four styles we also challenge and affirm all dimensions of thinking.

As we rotate our instruction across all four styles we simultaneously exercise students' perceptual capacities. Also, as we rotate our instruction through both interactive and cooperative groupings, as well as independent and self-reflective studies, we also affirm and challenge the attitudinal capacities of introversion and extraversion.

Compensation and Validation

Since our model is psychoanalytic, i.e., it looks at how the human psyche is structured and how it works, two primary Jungian ideas need clarification. The first of these is Jung's concept of compensation. Compensation has to do with what things (or behaviors) cost. When we require that students learn outside their own style we are insisting that they compensate, i.e., to expend higher levels of energy to learn outside of their own style, and to "pay" for their anxieties. The cost to the student takes the form of discomfort, irritability, boredom, unwillingness to participate, fear, self-perceived dullness, dependence on others, excessive talking, outright hostility, or low self-esteem. The price the student pays is suffering the negative recognition of others (peers, teachers, parents), and, also, the development of fears of learning. This latter fear is what Thorsten Veblen called "trained incapacities," i.e., the student learns what s/he believes to be skills they **can't** learn. Everyone compensates. Everyone is asked to perform tasks out of their dominant style. It's one thing for adults. We are already the result of our trained incapacities. But our relation to our students must be different. Where we were often denied the opportunity to develop all our learning capacities we are now in the position to offer more opportunities to our students. How do we undertake such an awesome task?

The response to the effects of students' inabilities to learn is Jung's notion of validation. To validate students is to continually affirm their capacities in their dominant style. The only way for the teacher to do this, authentically, is to teach required content in each style. This clearly requires compensatory behaviors on the teacher's part as well. Unlike children, however, our compensatory behaviors must not be allowed to be detrimental either to ourselves or others.

Teachers validate learners' capacities when any content is taught and tested in each style. Students are realists. To be validated in one's dominant style means to be recognized for some required academic achievement. It is not just recognition for effort; it is recognition for results. School is the real world for students. School grades are how students self-define learning capacity. To be validated in school is to be affirmed as being smart and worthy. The obverse is also, unfortunately, true. To not be validated means that one is invalidated. To be an "invalid," even if only as a self-recognition, is to be seen or to see oneself as ill, weak, or not normal. This is a burden students need not be asked to bear. It is a burden the society can no longer afford. There is a better way.

The Role of the Inferior Functions

The critical contribution this model makes in the thinking of teachers is in its recognition of the least-developed functions. These least-practiced functions are called inferior because they are not developed. Like any muscle group they only respond well when kept exercised. But the inferior functions are not dormant. Rather, the psyche demands wholeness of its possessor. To be whole means to be able to operate effectively and efficiently in **all** styles, **both** attitudes, and **both** orientations to closure. In effect the psyche's demands on its "owner" is that one becomes conscious, individuated, and self-aware. To resist the development of all one's functions and attitudes results in the loss

of "control" over one's life by the suppression of these psychic demands. Suppression means energy has been concentrated in the unacknowledged functions. This concentration of energy can't be contained by the conscious mind (since the conscious mind doesn't know it's there), and so it erupts, or takes on a mind of its own. Hence, the inferior functions run our lives through uncontrollable instincts and drives we experience but don't even know we possess. We only know we do things we don't want to do; don't do things we do want to do, and usually don't know what we're doing! Jung called the inferior functions "a loose and loaded cannon on the deck."

As teachers our responsibility to ourselves and our students is to use the model; to identify the roles of the inferior functions, to rotate instruction such that all students get to practice their least developed capacities, and to understand the inferior functions as the location of enormous energy for change. It is, then, from the undeveloped functions, that we get the energy to change, and the ability to be increasingly conscious. By continually exercising the inferior functions we reduce the need to compensate and simultaneously unload and secure the cannon.

Giving and Receiving Feedback

Learner profiles provide the teacher with essential information on how to provide feedback that both validates and challenges. In most cases the learner's dominant style will be opposite to the inferior or least developed style. Hence, to know the dominant for validation's sake, also offers insight for challenging in the inferior style. To validate a student's dominant style allows them to make positive assessments about their capacities as learners, and to be freer about trusting their perceptions. These positive teacher/learner assessments provide the rationale and ammunition to undertake what would otherwise be frightening tasks in the lesser-developed styles.

Key ideas to remember include:

STYLE	FEEDBACK	INTERVALS	THINKING OPERATION
ST dominant	• on accuracy and results	• frequent and quick	capacities for: • organizing for recall • demonstration of skills • sequences (steps in a process)
SF dominant	• on effort and involvement	• frequent and quick	capacities for: • search for personal relevance • self-expressive capacity • active listening skills • relating well to others • taking leadership roles • demonstrating empathy
NT dominant	• on critical/ analytical capacity • elegance and precision in reasoning	• infrequent but deliberate	capacities to: • analyze • synthesize • evaluate • make applications • defend a position • persuade • conduct research
NF dominant	• originality • creativity • "satisfying" applications	• infrequent and deliberate • aesthetic sense	capacities to create things that are insightful and beautiful, e.g., • works of art • dramatizations • paintings/illustrations • music and lyrics • projects/products • inventions • poetry • high level applications • social commentary • moral values

Providing consistent and positive feedback to students becomes a reality when all tasks are seen as "work in progress" and related to dominant capacity. Clearly, all students need to master all the skills represented by these four sets of thinking operations. Providing positive feedback in the student's dominant style allows the student to "hear" and accept your recommendations and questions in the lesser-developed styles.

Working Constructively With Resistance

Introduction

Students resist for their own reasons. In effect, all behavior is reasonable to the degree that it is necessary to take positions. The difference, of course, is in one's perspective and experience. As in working constructively with anger, the adult's first responsibility is to be clear about the student's reasons for being non-compliant or unresponsive. In effect the "need" to act-out, to rebel, to resist, is genuine. Resistance is, above all, a question of self-esteem or self-respect.

All of us resist. We resist because we are under some form of pressure to do well what we can't normally do. In "hostile" environments, e.g., classrooms for certain styles of learners, all of the defense mechanisms are called into operation because the student feels under siege. In effect the student is being attacked. The form of the siege, though often well-intentioned on the teacher's part, is to force the student to learn out of his/her own dominant style.

Since resistance is a normal and healthy behavior, the students that are acting-out are presenting us with a gift. Their resistance is their way of saying the instruction isn't working for them. As with the theory of Eastern martial arts the teacher will be most successful who uses the force of the resistance to improve instruction. Going with the force of the resistance recognizes both its power and its legitimacy!

When one's self-esteem is under attack, and that self-esteem is fragile at best, the psyche very naturally finds ways of diverting the pain or discomfort of the imposed perception on the self. Since the classroom, as a playing field, is not even due to the superordinate/sub-ordinate roles of teacher/student, the only "safe" way to protect oneself as a student is through resisting. In other words, too often the student can't say what s/he really thinks, or, more often, feels. So resistance is both a way to protect one's self-concept, and to not participate in what is seen as a demeaning process.

Hence the key to working creatively with resistance is to understand its motivation! Yes, there are reasons students resist! To know what these reasons are means we can use their force to teach more effectively. To resist the resistance is to end up in constant conflict.

What are students' needs that cause resistance? The phenomena needs to be understood on two levels: 1) the form of the challenge, and 2) the teacher's pre-emptive decision-making.

	STs	NTs	SFs	NFs
Student's need:	Competence	Challenge	Comfort	Coherence and elegance
Cause of resistance:	Feelings of incompetence	Feelings of inadequacy	Discomfort Irrelevance	The mundane and undemanding (lack of alternatives)
Teacher's pre-emptive decisions:	Provide for: clarity specificity factuality	Provide for: evidence argument conceptual clarity reasonableness	Provide for: expression of feeling support and cooperation verbalized learning	Provide for: aesthetic development alternative modes of learning expression of choice
Activities centers:	model the task drill & practice frequent feedback on accuracy discussion/recall	problem solving hypothesizing making connections debate reason	study groups coaching peer relationships teaming research dialogue relevance	projects/resources original work artistic activities dialectical method questions on moral issues

In effect to work with student resistance is to teach "around the wheel," to recognize that resistance is a natural defense mechanism, and to welcome its expression in order to apply it to students' growth and development.

Physical Settings and Student Groupings

The physical circumstances of our instructional space signal the styles of learning that are most likely going to take place. If the seats are in rows, it's very likely that the teacher will do most of the talking. If the chairs are in a circle, there's probably going to be opportunity for student talk. If the room is arranged around interest centers, there's probably going to be cooperative research efforts. If the furniture has been arranged around stations where students move from one to the other, there's probably going to be cooperative and collegial learning. Any type of teaching can occur with nearly any physical setting. But to facilitate curiosity and body movement, the furniture should be arranged to fit the style dominance of the task as nearly as possible. And, the kids love the variety.

Types of arrangements:

ST = focuses on efficiency, is businesslike, requires frequent quizzes and tests, and needs to process factual information quickly. Since the learning emphasis is on organizing information for recall, or performing a specific task, the learner sits passively. Organizing seats in rows with the teacher at the head of the class serves these functions well. Hence:

SF = focuses on peer partnerships, collaborative learning, coaching relationships, moving in and out of larger groups, heterogeneous groupings (both for ability levels and style dominance), jigsawing, and sharing scarce resources. This environment emphasizes verbalized learning, active listening, building group norms to facilitate class progress, sharing information, and developing improved self-awareness skills.

The physical arrangements call for flexible seating with access to tables or flat work spaces. Seats need to be movable so that students can work in pairs, triads, small and large group settings.

In this environment, the teacher serves as a facilitator and moves from grouping to grouping to monitor, serve as coach, or direct students to needed resources. The teacher's desk is usually in a corner. Hence:

NT = focus is on analysis, reasoning, research and hypothesizing. Teaching may be through group facilitation or lecture. Generally, the physical arrangement dramatizes the discussive or adversarial nature of critical learning. This format emphasizes debate, rhetoric and argument. Typically the class takes opposing sides. The room arrangement needs to be flexible to allow physical separation between the competing parties. Common forms for seating are sides at opposing tables, e.g., moot court, etc. In the NT position the underlying idea is that through argument and the analysis of multiple points of view, whatever truth there may be will be identified and distilled into a most defensible position. Hence:

NF = focus is on creative applications of required content in new and unusual forms. The portfolio and authentic assessment fall naturally into the NF position because of their focus on producing new products and projects, and on assessing the creative process over time. As students develop the content for their portfolios, a dialogue between teacher and students ensues as they analyze the changes students have made, as well as the merit of their productions.

The teacher's role is primarily that of modeler, facilitator, and resources person. Students' chairs are movable in order to access the variety of tools, materials, and work spaces available. Hence:

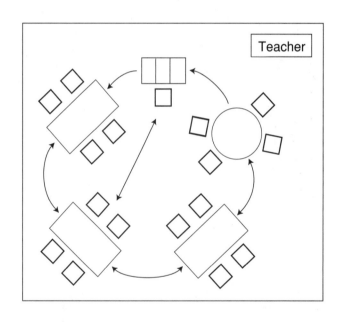

Making Homework Work

Homework is an essential aspect of the learning process, and style awareness is the critical component that can make homework an effective addition to student growth. We are defining homework as structured learning activities occurring outside of the classroom.

Making homework work is similar to inviting resistance and making preemptive decisions. When the teacher takes into consideration the needs of each style, and rotates homework over each of these sets of needs, then the work will be done that contributes to new learning.

What the style dominances need:

ST = Need the homework to be modelled in class; practice time in class must also be provided. The homework must be clear. Students should restate and write down the assignment to be accurate. The teacher needs to make a persuasive argument for why this particular piece of homework is necessary to learning. ST homework tends to focus on drill, practice, worksheets, workbooks, and correct, convergent and easily scored work.

SF = Need the homework to be modelled in class, but also need to do the practice items working in partnerships. SF's need time to practice and ask all their questions—whether of the teacher or a knowledgeable peer. To persuade the SF to do the homework, the teacher must be knowledgeable about real-world applications of the particular skills in work situations. Those relationships must be made clear and related to specific adult tasks and occupations. SF's need to practice the items, make mistakes, and get clarification on the nature of the tasks **before** taking the work out of the classroom. Unless there are restricting reasons why students shouldn't work together, the SF learns best in cooperative working relationships.

NT = Need the homework to be challenging and curiosity-provoking. NT's dislike rote and repetitious tasks. If NT's are asked to demonstrate the capacity to work certain math exercises, the number should be limited to the amount necessary to demonstrate competence. Five items of a similar type should be adequate.

NT's need homework where given a set of variables, they are asked to reach and defend a conclusion. Specific thinking skills that make homework interesting to the NT's are comparing and contrasting, identifying main ideas, making inferences, drawing conclusions, hypothesizing relationships, identifying patterns, and doing research. Written or verbal defenses of conclusions are the most satisfactory way of getting major ideas out quickly.

NF = Need the homework to be stimulating and evocative of their creative potential. NF's need to be challenged to expand, extend, and invent new relationships and applications. The homework needs to ask that existing content be reorganized and applied in creative and original ways. Homework alternatives should invite the uses of different forms of response, e.g., dramatizations, illustrations, role-plays, inventions, etc.

Regardless of the nature of the homework assigned, there must be assigned due dates. When that due date arrives, the teacher must have the students report on their homework, even if it means only handing in their work. Each assignment should be student-evaluated relative to its levels of difficulty, cogency, interest and overall applications to classwork. As students become more adept at evaluating the necessary roles of homework, they can assist in recommending both the types of homework to be done, and acceptable formats for presenting the completed homework, e.g., recitation, worksheets, essays, dramatizations, debates, or quick quizzes, etc.

Teachers must always have reasons for grading homework. Generally, homework is part of the practice entailed in learning some set of skills. Grading is not appropriate for practice. Self-assessment systems should be used for practice. Grading should be limited to evaluations of performance. All assessments leading up to performance should be for the purposes of improving instruction.

Styles, Strengths and Uses of Power

Introduction

Each dominant learning style has its own attendant strengths and applications of power.

Strengths are those tasks, skills, or activities that one does very well. Power is the application of those strengths for the purpose of getting others to do one's bidding.

Power can be exercised unconsciously as a defense against feeling powerless. As a defense mechanism, the exercise of power over others is a way of avoiding both one's feelings of powerlessness, and the demands of being in relationships with others.

Where power is exercised, there is no room for love, or the acceptance of others. Not being able to be in relationship with oneself, i.e., to accept oneself as one "truly" is means one controls others in order to avoid the pain of self-confrontation.

When power over others is exercised consciously, the judgment has been made that there is no time to resolve the problems at hand in more interdependent and collegial ways. While emergencies, real or imagined, may call for a hierarchy of decision-makers, the end effect is the separation of people, not the binding together. Relationships, both to oneself and to others, inevitably suffer when power is exercised as a conscious or unconscious preference.

Strengths and Powers

What one does well gives one a sense of satisfaction. Over time, one develops those skills and abilities to the place where, even to oneself, the exercise of those abilities seems relatively effortless. The unexamined assumption is that everyone values these abilities and, that, therefore, others should emulate one's own accomplishments. Thinkers, for instance, may be intolerant of feelers who disagree with the thinker's argument, but feel no need to come back with a counter-argument. Feelers can be equally judgmental toward thinkers contending that thinkers "…have no feelings." Sensors can be intolerant of intuitives by charging that the intuitors are vague, their heads are in the clouds, and they can't get their work done efficiently and on time. Intuitors view sensors as unimaginative, inflexible, and generally too involved in the immediate and concrete to see the larger picture.

Dominant styles tend to reflect power in the following ways:

ST's strengths include hard work, attention to detail, precision, efficiency, the pragmatic and the concrete. In school they tend to be neat, prompt, well-organized and to follow the rules. They accept the power structure and hierarchy of parents and teachers. In class they do the exercises in their workbooks, participate in drill and repetitive exercises and enjoy skill demonstrations in competitive and graded situations. They enjoy games, demonstrations, building things, and completing things.

Since power follows on strengths, STs exercise power by:

- identifying with adults
- competing successfully
- assuming leadership by directing others to the rules of the class or school, and
- struggling for position in peer hierarchies

STs tend to select regulatory roles in school, e.g., fire patrol, safety patrol, hall monitor, etc. Power comes from the emulation of authority and school/class rules. In the world of work, STs "run" organizations by using people to fulfill company goals.

NT's strengths include their analytical and evaluative abilities. They are the self-appointed skeptics. They are good at problem-solving, reading for information and meaning, organizing ideas, arguing various positions, and writing and speaking persuasively. In class they wait to speak until other ideas have been expressed. Then they simultaneously evaluate those ideas and provide their own conclusions. Their ability to withhold judgment and to listen critically allows them to make insightful summary judgments. They compare and contrast looking for key distinctions. They watch for exceptions to the rules. They have a keen eye for adult infractions of adult rules. They are perceived by the sensors as very wise and knowing—though the sensors might never admit it.

In classwork, the NTs write and speak well. They are voracious readers. They excel at writing essays, participating in debates and arguing. They enjoy the exercise of thought by playing the role of the devil's advocate. They enjoy independent study, research and logic problems.

Since power follows strength, the NTs exercise power by:

- citing their sources
- arguing and debating
- analyzing the weaknesses of others' points of view, and
- assuming the "high road" of superior knowledge

NTs tend to select evaluative roles in school, e.g., referee, judge, coach, mentor, etc. Their power is conferred on them by others as being more knowledgeable. NT's are put in leadership roles by those who want their actual or perceived critical thinking capacities. In the world of work, NTs tend to be the researchers, analysts, strategists, professors, teachers, scientists, etc. Their authority comes from their wisdom.

SF's strengths include their abilities to "read" people, to make friends, to sympathize, to express their feelings, to work effectively in groups, to make peace, to offer help in acceptable ways, and to support and encourage. In class they are mentors, coaches and teacher's aides. They enjoy getting peers to collaborate. They take personal responsibility for managing the class "grapevine," e.g., circulating information about what's happening to whom. They are good group members. They learn best in small interactive discussion settings.

In class, they work best in dyads and small discussion groups. They dislike competition. They are good in discussions because they ask the questions no one else will ask. They express their feelings as a way of keeping a discussion moving, and they can ask for help when they need it.

Since power follows strengths, the SFs exercise power by:

- being there when needed; being a friend
- sharing what they know, and don't know
- building networks
- being themselves

SFs have power placed on them by others. Their popularity leads to election to class offices. Their approachableness leads to their selection as leaders. Their power, in effect, is in their ability to reflect the group will. In the world of work, SFs tend to take high-level leadership positions because of their knowledge of how to work with all kinds of people.

NF's strengths include their abilities to originate, design, invent, compose, create, and to find and solve problems. Their interest in larger social problems and their resolution leads to a high moral consciousness. Their work is generally undertaken with enthusiasm because they tend to pursue their own feelings of interest. They become deeply involved in whatever project they're working on at the time. They are skillful at collecting and applying resources. Their ability to look at the familiar as strange, and the strange as familiar gives them unique perspectives on what to others are unimaginable. They use the arts to interpret social ills and the complexities of our existence.

In class, the NF excels at projects, the suggestion of alternative ways of learning and reporting on new tasks, the maintenance of logs and portfolios, and artistic endeavors of many different kinds. Peers tend to stand in awe of the creative NF, particularly where the NF's gifts are valued in a school setting, e.g., as a dancer, illustrator, musician, etc.

Since power follows strengths, the NFs exercise that power by:

• interpreting the meaningful in non-verbal (and verbal, e.g., poetry) ways

• being original, artistic and creative

• interpreting content and meaning in unusual ways

• carrying with them an "aura" of the ecstatic and sublime

NFs have power confirmed upon them by others. Other styles project onto the working NF special gifts. We admire their enthusiasm and independence. We envy their artistic abilities. We covet their special vocation and mission. Their power, in effect, is in their inspiration, their mission, their example. We give them power as our need to participate in their artistic insights. In the world of work, the successful NFs are designers, painters, novelists, poets, philosophers, theologians, and inventors. They tweak our noses while they simultaneously pique our curiosity. Other dominant styles want to do what they do without becoming what they are.

Hook and Hold: Questions, Tasks, Anticipatory Sets, Assessment and Time Over All Four Styles

Introduction

The fundamentally important idea of simultaneously affirming and challenging all styles of learning is critical to students' mastery of required content, and to their psychological development. This idea is realized in the classroom when teachers practice the hook and hold concept.

"Hooking" is the way we get students' attention. "Holding" is the way we keep it. When a teacher hooks one style of learner, the other styles may be turned off. Similarly, to hold one style of learner because instruction is consonant with their style is to simultaneously lose the opposing styles. In effect, only by rotating each of the dimensions of the strategy can the teacher reach all learners.

The dimensions of hook and hold are:

1. The use of anticipatory sets, e.g., warm-ups, getting the kids turned on

2. Tasks—The content to be learned segmented into their style-alike pieces

3. Questions—The asking of questions to evoke different kinds of thinking, and

4. Assessment—The kinds of questions, tasks, and assignments we use to alert students to their progress through required content.

The metaphor for hook and hold is to "teach around the wheel." The wheel has a rim and spokes. The rim represents the needs/abilities of the four styles. The spokes represent the four dimensions. Hence:

TEACHING AROUND THE WHEEL

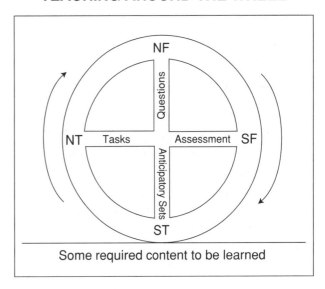

Some required content to be learned

Anticipatory sets as style issues:

A good anticipatory set has something in it for each style of learner.

ST = What is to be learned and how tested, e.g., clarity, specificity, accountability. The teacher presents the objectives, explains the practice, and sets times for performance.

NT = The teacher asks questions that stimulate curiosity or the solving of problems. The learner's interest is piqued by answering the question.

SF = The teacher tells a story or asks about the learners' experiences that are parallel to the content of the lesson. The anticipatory set establishes a basis for empathy or self-understanding.

NF = The teacher challenges the learner to make new and original applications.

Generally, the form of the anticipatory set is as a question, story or task. Good sets meet these criteria:

1. Stimulate curiosity (ST, NT)
2. Reduce anxiety, e.g., fears about not being able to learn the new content (SF)
3. Ignite the imagination (NF).
4. Set context for lesson, and
5. Appeal to all styles

Tasks as style issues:

Integrating activities and assignments from all style positions increase students' accessibility to the learning.

ST = Convergent, true/false, factual, the demonstration of sequences, recitation, skill development

NT = Analytical, reasonable, evidential, evaluative, inferential, demonstrations of critical applications of reading

SF = Cooperative, collegial, emphasize verbal interaction, sharing, team membership, leadership, coaching

NF = Looking for alternatives, creative, new applications, artistic, inventive, entrepreneurial

The issue with tasks by styles is to isolate within a lesson the components that are style dependent, e.g.,

ST = facts, sequences, and demonstrations

NT = arguments, comparisons, conclusions

SF = involvement, commitment, and verbal interaction

NF = applications, innovations, interpretations

By rotating the lesson's tasks over each of the styles, the content has been taught more broadly and deeply. Each style has been affirmed and challenged.

Questions as style issues:

The way we ask questions determines how we want students to think. To think in each of the positions means we rotate our questions.

ST = Who, what, when, where, and sometimes how. How is an ST question when it asks the student to repeat a practiced skill. ST questions focus on accuracy, sequence, and demonstrability. Answers are convergent and quickly verifiable.

NT = How, in the sense of solving a problem not previously practiced; also why. Most NT questions take the form of tasks, e.g., compare and contrast, evaluate, summarize, induce, deduce, hypothesize, etc. NT questions focus on the most defensible responses. NT tasks rely on research, citations of evidence, and persuasive capacity.

SF = "What has your experience been?" Sometimes "how do you feel about...?" SF questions have to do with feelings, personal experiences, self-awareness and self-concept, and the ability to see relationships between their experience and the relevance of the content they're being asked to learn.

NF = "What might have happened if…?" Also, as with the NT question, the question is in the form of a directive, e.g., draw, sculpt, paint, dramatize, invent, alter, imagine, etc. The NF questions ask students to make real-world applications of the content in order to demonstrate their integration and understanding of that content.

Rotating one's questions around the styles requires advanced preparation. Since all forms of questions are essential to the success of all learners, teachers need to practice these skills until they are virtually automatic.

Assessment as a style issue

Assessment is for the specific purpose of alerting students to what they actually know and can demonstrate about the required content. Assessment is for the on-going purposes of providing frequent feedback on personal progress. The teacher assumption that underlies this effort is the need for both teachers and students to know where one is in a learning process all the time.

Assessment is not performance. Assessment is to practice as grading is to performance. Assessment is for the purpose of teaching and learning. Performance is for the purpose of grading or evaluation. Assessment is a formative approach to learning where there are frequent feedback loops and opportunities to correct errors and mistakes. Assessment's purpose is to have all learners be academically and personally successful.

Performance is a summative approach which has as its sole purpose the evaluation of the degrees to which tasks have been mastered. Summative evaluation is the end of the line. Grades are issued.

Formative assessments in the aggregate predict very accurately the summative performance.

ST = Emphasis on recall, demonstration and accuracy

NT = Emphasis on elegance of the argument, citation of evidence and reasoning processes

SF = Emphasis on involvement, articulation of ideas and feelings, and relating content to one's own life experiences

NF = Emphasis on making applications demonstrating deep understanding

The two feeling (F) assessment positions require additional time (SF) and access to resource materials (NF).

Designing Lessons "Around The Wheel"

Introduction

A balanced or integrated unit/lesson is any set of instructional procedures that:

- accomplishes specific objectives or outcomes
- contains learning activities for each of the outcomes across each of the four styles
- arranges for the processing of content in both active (extrovert) and reflective (introvert) ways
- promotes thinking through the asking of ST and NT questions
- promotes self-reflection and creativity by asking SF and NF questions
- assesses in all four styles
- evaluates in all four styles, and
- has portfolio requirements falling in all four styles

The teacher's challenge in designing such lessons or units is in getting the balance of tasks, activities and assessments that will most effectively help every style of learning to master the content within the required timeframe.

The key issue for planning, implementation and evaluation is balance. Where the four sets of style capacities are relatively equally balanced the integration of emphases that will result will guarantee higher levels of student involvement and accomplishment.

Sample Lessons

We've included five sample lessons as indications of what can be accomplished by integrating all the style dimensions.

The first lesson's purpose is to facilitate students' abilities to write coherent paragraphs. The strategy utilized is called Pass Around Paragraph. Its applications are generally elementary and middle-school level. It's very useful for remediation/skill development at all levels.

In Pass Around Paragraph the ST task is to:

- write to the point
- use correct spelling, grammar and punctuation
- form letters legibly
- build on the prior sentence

In the SF style all learners are expected to:

- participate in the group discussion
- share ideas and feelings
- coach one another and make suggestions, and
- help peers who are having difficulty

In the NT style the learners must:

- analyze the problem
- evaluate alternatives
- look for patterns or possibilities, and
- hypothesize or find connections

In the NF position students must write a constructive and persuasive paragraph that demonstrates:

- a basic knowledge of the topic
- shows some creativity in expression
- demonstrates the use of metaphor, and
- uses appropriate modifiers for verbs and nouns

The lesson (may take more than one period) is then concluded by:

- posting each group's work
- having teams compare and contrast the paragraphs
- identify dominant similarities/differences, and
- participate in a large group discussion on what they learned about themselves and the content using the Pass Around Paragraph strategy

---

PASS AROUND PARAGRAPH
Sample Lesson: Writing Coherent Paragraphs

Pass Around Paragraph is a cooperative writing activity that reinforces the direct teaching of basic paragraph structure. It can be used with pairs of students, triads or groups of four.

Steps:
1. Begin with a topic sentence. This can be teacher-generated or developed by the group. One student in the group copies the topic sentence on the paper

Example: Planning ahead for a garage sale is important.

2. The topic sentence is passed to a second student in the group who adds a detail sentence.

3. The paper is then passed to the third student who adds another detail sentence.

4. The fourth student in the group adds the final detail sentence.

5. The paragraph is passed back to student #1. This student writes a concluding statement that the whole group has agreed upon.

6. Pass Around Paragraphs are shared with the class.

A second example is any lesson where the content is processed in a discussion, large or small group format, and where four sets of participation skills are to be practiced. This strategy is called Active Listening and the skills are broken down by styles.

As the teacher teaches the lesson time is allotted for the practice of the specific skills of active listening.

Teachers should introduce the skills, one at a time, over several weeks. The teacher needs to model each of the skills before assigning practice. When the skills are being introduced, it's appropriate to call on volunteers.

After the skills have been practiced for several days then students can be called on; by the teacher, by peers, by names from a hat, by numbers, etc.

Learning the Active Listening skills adds to each student's learning repertoire and vastly facilitates understanding, empathy and retention.

ACTIVE LISTENING
Sample Lesson: A Process for Learning to Listen Well

A strategy to increase attention, to develop critical thinking skills, to facilitate class growth and ownership of learning, and to make students aware of one another's feeling states.

INTRODUCTION:
Active listening is a set of learned skills. They can only be learned through practice. The teacher is encouraged to introduce the skills one-by-one and to arrange the practice of the skills over time, e.g., one per week for nine weeks. The strategies also correlate to capacities by styles. Most instruction tends to make heavy use of the ST and NT skills and to neglect the SF and NF.

Active listening assumes a relationship between students where learning is seen as collaborative and self-sustaining. When the active listening skills have been integrated into the student's repertoire, higher achievement occurs on both the content and the interpersonal levels. The skills are as follows:

Sensing-Thinking (ST)—practical and concrete

1. Paraphrasing—the ability to correctly condense and restate the essence of what someone has said, and then to ask for feedback, i.e., "Was my paraphrase correct?", or "Was that what you meant?" Paraphrasing is not listing, it's not sequencing, and it's not a summary. Paraphrasing is the correct rehearsal of what was said to the extent that it is approved by the speaker. In paraphrasing there is no evaluation of the speaker's content.

2. Data-gathering or clarification—the ability to ask for data in order to be clear about what's being said, or, if confused by what is said to politely ask for clarification or restatement.

Sensing-Feeling (SF)—self-awareness and interpersonal response

3. Perception-checking—the ability to "read" peoples' facial and body language, i.e., to interpret what's happening within a person and then by asking if your perception is what the person is actually experiencing, e.g., if the person is sitting cross-armed and crossed-legged with a frown the perception might be, "Mary, are you angry about what's being said?", or, "John, are you very disappointed by what's happening?", etc. Every perception check must be followed by a request for feedback, i.e., "Is that how you're feeling?" Perception checks must always be in the form of questions in order that they not be perceived as judgments, but rather as requests for involvement.

4. Personal Sharing—the ability to "build" on what a prior speaker has said as a way of inviting rapport and of enhancing the discussion. Personal sharing, usually as an "I" message, relates a meaningful prior experience to the content of the discussion. Its purpose is to demonstrate interest and empathy.

continued on next page

continued from previous page

Intuitive-Thinking—critical, analytical and conceptual thinking

5. Evaluating-critiquing—the ability to identify standards or measures and to assess the discussion content critically against these measures. Verbal protocols invite statements, such as, "As I understand it you're saying…, but I think… because…." Evaluating statements are not rebuttals, but are rather arguments for an alternative view based on announced standards or criteria. A useful protocol in a strenuous argument might be, "Bill, you and I may have to agree to disagree," or, "While I like your summary I can't agree with your conclusion," etc. The evaluative comment only facilitates group understanding when the evaluator cites reason for his conclusion. The critical word is "because". Most arguments can be resolved once there is agreement on the relevant facts and the standards for evaluation.

6. Summarizing—the ability to fairly condense a discussion's content into its most important ideas and facts, followed by the request for feedback, i.e., "Is this the group's interpretation?" or, "Have I hit all the main points?"

7. Opining—the ability to share an opinion as the result of reflecting on the discussion's content, and to verbalize the opinion as data for discussion. The flavor of the opine is to stimulate more thought, to be constructively provocative, rather than in the sense of, "Well, the fact of the matter is…," or, "The real issue is…," or, "No mater what anyone said I believe…," etc.

Intuitive-feeling—creative, innovative and original interpretation

8. Headlining—the ability to grasp the inner essence of a topic and condense it into an alliterative or rhyming phrase. Headlines must catch the whole idea in just four or five words. Headlining requires metaphorical and imaginative thinking to create word plays, alliterations or clear images, e.g., a local winemakers group met recently with new membership. The headline read Grape Group Grows, etc. The best headliners are sports writers! Headlining must be taken seriously as a skill since the capacity to retain meaning in a few words is an essential memory skill task.

9. Alternative scenarios—the ability to create divergent and alternative endings to stories, situations or problems. Creative scenarios require imagination, drawing mental pictures, following through on a sequence to "see" how it turns out, and imagining ideal states. In imagining ideal states the thinker assumes optimal conditions, few or no limitations, and then designs the ideal. The capacity to design alternatives is the essence of the creative and critical thinking act. It represents the capacity to see "what is" while simultaneously designing "what needs to be."

STEPS

1. The teacher establishes a schedule for introducing the active listening skills

2. The teacher, in facilitating discussion, introduces the skills, role models the skill, and explains the schedule.

3. During the discussion either the teacher may call upon a student to practice the skill, or students may be invited to call on other students to demonstrate the skill. Calling should be random. Summarizing, evaluating, headlining and scenario creation cannot occur until the discussion is well enough underway to provide the needed content for practice.

4. As the practice weeks go by both teacher and students should practice a "mix" of the skills.

5. The teacher needs to monitor the process so that all students practice all the skills.

6. The teacher, or a student, facilitates a class discussion over how the active listening skills enhance concentration, learning, and retention.

A third approach to teaching around the wheel is in distributing required learning over all four styles and at different levels of difficulty. We call this design process lesson or unit menus.

The purpose of unit menus is to allow students choices, while at the same time covering the required skills. Students must complete the outcomes on all the levels but can decide the sequence to be followed, and how to schedule their time.

UNIT MENUS
Sample Lesson on conic sections and Romeo and Juliet

A strategy that incorporates Task Rotation, Graduated Difficulty and learning profile development in order to simultaneously teach higher order thinking skills and the development of all the styles within one's profile.

Introduction:
Unit menus are teacher designed. They are sets of choices offered to students on both levels of difficulty and style preferences. However, as in the Task Rotation strategy, they also require that the student select across levels of difficulty and style.

Generally, the menu is a 3 x 4 or 4 x 4 matrix. The horizontal dimension represents the task broken down by style dominances, i.e., ST-Mastery, NT-Understanding, SF-Inter/Intrapersonal, and NF-Self Expressive/Synthesis.

The vertical axis represents levels of difficulty. How many levels of difficulty are to be offered is the teacher's choice. Sometimes teacher choice is constrained by the content, e.g., adding two digit numbers, or spelling words. At other times the content may demand three, four or five levels of understanding and application, e.g. interpreting the novels of James Joyce, or making real world applications of polynomials.

Designing menus is hard work. The motivation to do so is compelling, however, since the menu presents an elegant and comprehensive description of the content to be learned. The menu also guides the student through a richer, deeper, and more challenging learning experience than they would otherwise have had.

The unit menu also represents an enlightened approach to authentic assessment, because it requires that the student process the required content as recall, reason, reflections on personal relevance, and then to reorganize and apply the data to a real world problem.

The student's selection process within the menu also provides both teacher and learner with ongoing assessment data relative to competence and progress. The student may then ask for the help that's needed and/or the teacher can reteach the content in a different style, or on a different level.

Steps:
1. The teacher selects the content to be learned by:
- analyzing skills by style
- identifying the higher order thinking skills to be demonstrated
- utilizing the matrix for Designing Graduated Menus
- studying the sample menus.

2. The teacher then designs a matrix across the four styles and according to the requisite number of levels of difficulty.

3. The teacher then determines what choices the students may make, e.g.,
- one task at each level
- one task on every level by style
- any level at a style of one's choosing, etc.

Note: The rule of thumb on a 3 x 4 matrix is that the student select a different style on three levels of difficulty, hence, e.g., ST-level I, NT-level II, NF-level

III, etc. A 4 x 4 menu is ideal because the student may respond on every level and in every style.

4. The teacher field tests the menu to see if:
- the student can function at all levels
- the way the content has been designed for teaching addresses the levels of difficulty and styles
- The students' work represents both high levels of competence and challenges students to think in all four positions.

5. Students then select, according to the teacher's directions, the styles and levels at which they will work.

6. The teacher explains that completed work on, say, level three or level four is necessary to master the material. Taken a step further, all level four work across all four styles could be an A; all level three work across all styles could be a B, etc.

LEARNING STYLES AND QUESTIONING STYLES
Conic Section Menu: Bite into a few activities

Directions: You should complete four assignments for this unit. Choose one from each difficulty level for a total of three. Then choose your fourth from whatever difficulty level you want. The tricky part of this is that each of your choices must be from a different learning style.

Difficulty Level	Mastery	Understanding	Self-Expressive	Interpersonal
1	Draw a picture of all of the conic sections. Label each one.	A circle is very similar to an ellipse, yet it does not have a major or minor axis. Why?	Self-Expressive Using a flashlight, create a "shadow show" for your classmates that lets you demonstrate your knowledge of conic sections (e.g. could you make the image of a circle on the wall? A parabola?).	For each conic section put a ☺ (I feel good) or a ☺ (I have a question). Have your teacher help you answer your questions. Work until you can put a ☺ next to each conic section.
				*If you have a ☺ next to each at the start, you should choose a Level 2 or Level 3 activity instead.
2	Make a list of 8 important terms to know from this unit. Define each.	Compare and contrast the equations for conic sections. Create a list of 10 "masterful tips" that could help a confused classmate tell apart and memorize them easier.	Perform a play with a cast that includes: **Mr./Ms. Circle** **Mr./Ms. Ellipse** **Mr./Ms. Parabola** **Mr./Ms. Hyperbole** Be sure that each character describes him/herself.	Select the conic section that best illustrates how you feel. Draw it and explain why you chose that particular shape.
3	Sketch the following conic sections: $\frac{x^2}{25} + \frac{y^2}{9} = 1$ $y = \frac{1}{8}y^2$ $\frac{x^2}{16} - \frac{y^2}{9} = 1$ Label each sketch.	Find a simple physics textbook and look up the topic "projectile motion." What conic section is involved in projectile motion. How? Write a paragraph that shares what you learned.	Create a song or rap that includes two or more formulas that describe conic sections.l	Play the "Art Game" with a partner. Play each role at least twice and submit your "art" to your teacher.

THOUGHTFUL EDUCATION
Romeo & Juliet Assignment Menu

Directions: You must complete four assignments for this unit. Choose one from each difficulty level, and one from each learning style.

Difficulty Level	Mastery	Understanding	Self-Expressive	Interpersonal
1	Choose three unfamiliar vocabulary words from each act (total of 15). Write the word, a definition, and sentence.	Explain what possible solutions the Prince could have come up with early in the play to solve the problems the town and the two families were having.	Complete an "Open Mind" for Romeo or Juliet. Include a short written explanation for your symbols.	What advice do you give Romeo when you run into him in the street? **OR** You are old Montague. What advice do you give to Juliet when you run into her in the street?
2	Create a timeline of the play's major events. Use a long piece of paper or four or more regular sheets so the timeline is large enough to see if it is put on the classroom wall. **OR** Find an example for each of the following: pun, personification, simile, metaphor, allusion—explain your example.	What happened to Romeo and Juliet probably wouldn't have happened if only… Find three places in the play where you would have had something different happen that would change the outcome of the play. Explain what could have happened, and what effect it would have had on the play's outcome.	Find a partner or partners and choose a portion of the play that you can perform in about 3-5 minutes. Rehearse carefully and perform for the class. **OR** If you wish to perform alone, find an important speech from the play and perform for the class.	Interview all of the students in class on their views of suicide. Write up the results of your interviews; give a brief presentation of your findings to the class.
3	Make a list of the play's archaic words and a modern equivalent. Your list should include at least 45 words. **OR** Look up Echo, The Titans, Phaeton, and write a report on these mythical figures alluded to in the play.	Defend the statement some critics have made that Romeo acts foolishly and is responsible for the play's tragic conclusion. Prepare an argument that defends his actions. **OR** Do some research and write a report about the 14th century, looking especially for information that pertains to the play.	Write a song for Romeo and Juliet. Record, videotape or perform your song; an alternative is to find a group that fits the style of your lyrics, play one of their songs then explain to the class what your song would sound like if they did it. **OR** Choose 3-5 important lines from the play and illustrate them with your own artwork.	Write four letters between any two characters in the play. The play starts on Sunday and ends early Thursday morning. The letters should reflect the events taking place, so date them. **OR** Write a daily journal (diary) entry for one of the characters for each day of the play.

Still another approach to unit design is to present to students some outcome or project to be constructed. Using a strategy called Jurying the students prepare to do exemplary work by:

- functioning in teams (SF)

- analyzing and evaluating (NT)

- determining and practicing the skills (ST), and

- creating exemplary projects demonstrating how they have mastered the content and have made creative applications (NF)

Jurying, as a strategic process, works with all age groups and is a natural way to simultaneously reduce anxiety about expectations, and to promote high level critical and creative outcomes.

JURYING
Sample Lesson on Setting Standards

A strategy to involve students in the assessment of their own learning through the setting and prioritizing of the criteria for work to be performed and for the grades to be awarded.

Introduction:
Jurying is a critical strategy for every teacher's repertoire! Jurying is the essential beginning point for any unit of instruction. It is a strategy that builds an understanding of and commitment to the learning of any new body of material or practice.

Jurying is also an essential step in the implementation of authentic assessment, the setting of standards, criteria, benchmarks or rubrics, the mastery demonstrations of required skills, and the description of such content as shall be collected in students' portfolios and journals.

The students' involvement in this standard-setting strategy invites not only ownership of the content, but also clear explanation for how performance is to be assessed and graded. On the teacher's part, jurying, as an involvement and clarifying strategy, makes possible an understanding of students' needs, the capacity to anticipate necessary interventions (i.e., alternative ways of teaching the content), and to gain the clarity necessary for a just and fair notation and grading system.

The steps in this strategy are generic and apply to the introduction of all new content. Each step is also accompanied by a set of protocols. Protocols are verbal (or written) statements that clarify the purpose(s) for each step. Their intent is to teach, through repetition and practice, planning and implementation skills; e.g., embodied within the protocols are the skills of analysis (see Compare and Contrast, Conclude and Defend), induction (see Inductive Learning), deduction (see Concept Attainment), inference (see Reading for Meaning), evaluation (see Summarize and Praise), organization (see Visual Organizers or new American Lecture), and creative thinking (see Creative Thinking, Torrancial Thinking, or Metaphorical Problem Solving).

Steps:
Jurying follows, as in the world of work or litigation, the following steps:

1. Students are shown several (at least three) **exemplary** or **distinguished** models, examples or demonstrations of what the materials or skills are to look like in their final form. In this first phase the student observes, compares and contrasts, concludes, defends observations, identifies key attributes of the content, etc. This observation phase needs to last long enough, or to be repeated often enough, so that every learner can perceive and ingest the material thoroughly. The protocols in this first phase are admonitions to look carefully, take time to be thorough, share your observations with others, explore likes and dislikes, etc.

continued on next page

continued from previous page

2. Students next are asked to **analyze** what the exemplary models or demonstrations have in common. The protocols include testing hypotheses, arguing alternative interpretations, building consensus, gaining clarity by asking one's own questions, etc. In this second phase students list the attributes that all the exemplary models share. A list is prepared where everyone can see. Items are not added to the list until every student sees how the item is common to all the models. The teacher facilitates this process and directs students' attention to those items they may have missed. This phase in which the teacher adds items is critical of understanding exemplary standards. The teacher needs to take the time for students to understand how the new items are common to all the models.

3. Students now are broken into heterogeneous teams to put the attributes of the exemplary models into an order of importance or criticality. Clearly all of the commonalities are not of equal significance. The process is one in which teams nominate certain items/attributes that are critical to exemplary work. The protocol is for a student to name an attribute as essential and to give reasons for that selection. The student might say, "I nominate item #5 because it is common to all three models and because it seems to represent the central purpose of the poem, short story, science project, etc." Having nominated the item the students then rank, based on a 1 (lowest) to 5 (highest) scale, the nominations. The groups' rankings are then added up and divided by the number of students in the group. This simple averaging system provides each item discussed with its own rank within the group. This ranking then facilitates the whole class ranking since the teacher or facilitator can invite all items ranked at 4 or more, etc., to begin the final and whole class ranking process. In the whole class setting the teacher arbitrates the weighting process by questioning students' thinking and by asking for evidence.

4. In this fourth phase the student teams are asked, initially by the teacher and later on by the students themselves, to **identify** as specifically as possible where the highest ranked items are found in the exemplary models or demonstrations. This is an essential phase in the students' understanding of standards or criteria. Often, the critical attributes of a work are not easily identified, must be inferred, and may cover, in the aggregate, various aspects of a work; e.g., how an author builds suspense, the form the humor takes, flashes of insight into human behavior, development of plot and character, etc. The teacher's uses of the protocols at this stage require both analytical and affective uses of the language; e.g., often aesthetic dimensions of outstanding fiction have large like/dislike components (one likes Huck Finn's dishonesty, because the larger good is in helping Jim escape, for example). It is the liking or disliking, as a feeling state, that builds and holds interest. The classics are classic because for most readers, and over a very long period of time, people are still engaged by the author's capacity to sound certain recurring themes in human experience. The aesthetic dimension of a literary work, a math equation, or a science project is in its elegance. Elegance is the "fit" perceived between the analytical and affective responses of the reader or user. It is in this fourth phase that the teacher directs learners to look more deeply, to see new connections and to experience the beauty of what is being learned. It is in this aesthetic dimension of learning as interaction between content and personal experience that allows for expressions of understanding and appreciation.

5. In the fifth step the teacher **role models**, **demonstrates**, or performs any highly ranked item for which clarification is needed. The protocols work best in peer groups where, after steps 1 through 4 have been completed, students can share with one another their points of confusion. The protocol is to invite the confusion; i.e., that learning anything new brings some confusion and that confusion is, in itself, a sign that learning is taking place. In other words, one learns to know what one does not know.

When the teams come back together to ask for clarification on confusing items the teacher facilitates the best ways to provide the missing information; i.e., to get other students to respond, to return to the exemplary models, to answer oneself, etc. Since jurying asks, as its primary intent, that the student master the material at a very high level, all questions need to be addressed before moving on to step #6.

continued on next page

continued from previous page

6. The teacher, through directed questioning, leads students to a clear understanding of how the ranked criteria, represented in the exemplary models or demonstrations, indicated "distinguished" or A-level work.

Directed questioning, a verbal protocol, walks students through the previously ranked criteria, one by one, to indicate how in the aggregate each exemplary model reflects those same criteria.

7. The next step is to have students do the assigned work, reflecting on all the previously determined criteria.

8. The final step is to have students read, critique, or *jury* one another's work, again applying the criteria and assigning notations.

Notations are specific comments on the paper, project or performance, referencing the use or absence of each of the criteria. The teacher spot-checks to see that the criteria are being used objectively.

The papers or projects are then returned to the authors to make necessary revisions. Once the work has been revised it is again distributed to another student to read and critique. Students need to make sure they have a different reader for the second critique. The papers are again returned to the author for final revisions. Again, the teacher will want to spot-check the second revisions to make sure students are jurying their peers' work fairly and according to the predetermined criteria.

Some General Notes:
• Juried work needs to represent the Unit's most important learnings.

• Criteria development for most important and higher level work will generally take several run-throughs before the standards are as comprehensive and clear as is necessary for students to do uniformly high quality work.

• Students need time to fully appreciate their roles in criteria development, executing work responsive to criteria, jurying or critiquing a peer's work, and the drafting and revision process.

Some Predictable Outcomes:
Students will be:
1) more involved in learning through their participation in the design process

2) able to do higher level and more demanding work

3) able to explain the multiple uses of criteria

4) able to accurately predict their notation levels and final grades

5) able to give their peers constructive feedback on their work

Our last example is a sample unit on prejudice using a strategy called Task Rotation.

In this unit teachers use a combination of strategies to help students process the task in different styles. The participating strategies are:

- Dyads—students working in pair/share arrangements (SF)

- Drill, practice and memorization (of the poem) (ST)

- Thinking about a prior event in one's life (SF)
- Reading and analyzing the poem "Incident" (NT)
- Interpreting the poem (reading for meaning) (NT)
- Metaphor (how are the qualities of prejudice like a tree, shadow, etc. (NF)
- Writing a creative essay (NT/NF)

Task Rotation as a strategy works on any content where the teacher wants extended cognitive and affective involvement.

TASK ROTATION
(Teaching Around The Wheel)

Introduction:
Task Rotation is a strategy for learning important content in depth. Depth is achieved by learning the content in each of the four style positions, i.e., Mastery learning for facts and procedures; Understanding learning for concepts and critical analysis; Inter/intrapersonal learning for self-concept and expression of feelings and values, and Self-Expressive learning for creative and original applications of the content, i.e., what the student can do with what's been learned.

Steps:
1. The teacher identifies the unit's major objective(s) and designs assignments in each of the four positions.

2. The teacher explains that the Self-expressive assignment is left until the last but that otherwise they can choose where they would like to begin. Choice comes with the understanding that they must complete all four assignments by the unit's completion.

3. The teacher facilitates discussion on how choices were made.

4. See Menus.

THE ONCE AROUND:
Welcome To The Foyer

Sample Lesson

Think about an important event in your life... how were things different after? What was the turning point? In the space below write down some of your feelings and impressions.

A Turning Point... An Incident

_____

_____

_____

_____

_____

_____

_____

_____

_____

_____

_____

_____

_____

_____

_____

_____

_____

_____

_____

_____

_____

_____

_____

_____

_____

_____

_____

_____

ONCE AROUND IN LITERATURE:
Focusing On The Poem's Structure

This picture of a slide represents the structure of the poem. The left bubble represents the character's feelings before the incident. The bubble at the top of the slide represents the incident or the "turning point." It shows the point when things change. The right bubble represents the character's feelings afterward.

Read the poem that follows and fill in the bubbles.

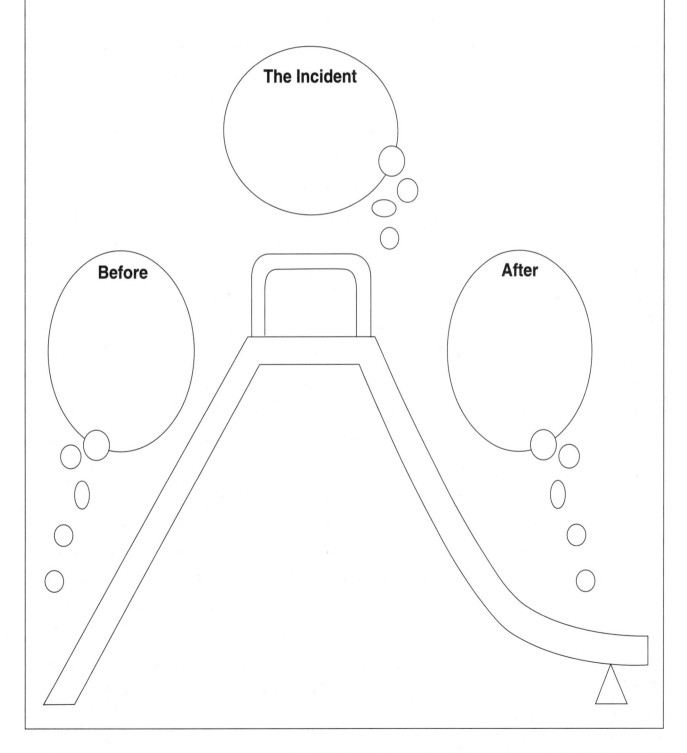

Incident

by Countee Cullen

Once riding in old Baltimore,

Heart-filled, head-filled with glee,

I saw a Baltimorean

Keep looking straight at me.

Now I was eight and very small,

And he was no whit* bigger,

And so I smiled, but he poked out

His tongue, and called me, "Nigger."

I saw the whole of Baltimore

From May until December;

Of all the things that happened there

That's all that I remember.

*"Whit"—"the least bit, jot; iota: chiefly in negative construction (not a whit the wiser)" from Webster's New World Dictionary, Third College Edition, Simon and Schuster, Inc. 1988.

READING FOR MEANING

Agree   or   **Disagree**   **The boy saw all of Baltimore**
☐   ☐   What are your reasons for agreeing or disagreeing?

_____

_____

_____

_____

_____

Agree   or   **Disagree**   **The language of the poem is too simple**
☐   ☐   What are your reasons for agreeing or disagreeing?

_____

_____

_____

_____

_____

Agree   or   **Disagree**   **The incident was completely destructive**
☐   ☐   What are your reasons for agreeing or disagreeing?

_____

_____

_____

_____

_____

Agree   or   **Disagree**   **Confronting prejudice made the boy stronger**
☐   ☐   What are your reasons for agreeing or disagreeing?

_____

_____

_____

_____

_____

PLANNING FOR MEMORY

Develop a plan to help you memorize this poem.

First…

_____

_____

_____

_____

_____

_____

Then…

_____

_____

_____

_____

_____

_____

Next…

_____

_____

_____

_____

_____

_____

Last…

_____

_____

_____

_____

_____

_____

PREJUDICE IS LIKE...

Countee Cullen, the author of "Incident", did not include any similes in his poem. Create a simile about prejudice that he might have been able to use in "Incident" or in another poem about prejudice. You can use any of the suggested similes at the bottom of the page or you can create your own. (If you create your own, have your teacher approve it before going on.) Once you have created your simile, fill in the chart that follows.

Prejudice is like a(n) _____ .

(fill in the blank)

Qualities of Prejudice	Qualifies of _____ (the object you picked)
1. *It can show up where you don't expect it to.*	1. _____
2. _____	2. _____
3. _____	3. _____
4. _____	4. _____
5. _____	5. _____
6. _____	6. _____
7. _____	7. _____
8. _____	8. _____
9. _____	9. _____
10. _____	10. _____

Suggestions:
Prejudice is like a(n) _____ .

tree	shadow	ice cube	roller coaster
mirror	jigsaw puzzle	whale	

ESSAY PLANNER

Are you ready to write another short essay? Do you remember the thesis—evidence—conclusion format? Use the chart below to help you remember the format and to help you plan your essay.

Thesis: A thesis is a statement that you will try to prove. For this essay, your simile will be your thesis. It is what you will try to prove. Write your thesis here.

_____

_____

_____

_____

_____

Evidence: Evidence is the information that you find to support and prove your thesis. Look back at the chart that lists the qualities of prejudice and the qualities of the object you chose. How are they similar? List the similarities here.

_____

_____

_____

_____

_____

_____

Conclusion: A conclusion ties your essay together. Was your simile a good one? How did you know? Write your conclusions here.

_____

_____

_____

_____

_____

Your whole essay is now planned out. Use the lined page that follows to write a rough draft. Once you have created your rough draft, reread your essay to see if there is anything that you want to change or correct. Then write your final draft.

continued on next page

continued from previous page

ESSAY

_____

_____

_____

_____

_____

_____

_____

_____

_____

_____

_____

_____

_____

_____

_____

_____

_____

_____

_____

_____

_____

_____

_____

_____

_____

_____

_____

_____

_____

_____

_____

9

CHAPTER NINE

Learning Styles As Reflections Of Needs And Attitudes

Introduction

The pursuit of self-knowledge is a never-ending process. How vigorously we pursue a better understanding of ourselves has profound implications for our work with students and peers. To be eager to grow; to know more about ourselves; to become more aware of how we choose some behaviors and reject others, and how we compensate for our perceived weaknesses is the stuff of which mature, well-integrated personalities are made.

Jung called this state of integration or maturity the process of individuation. The individuating person is the one who is aware of his preferences, his attitudes, and his need to be able to operate laterally with "confluence" depending on the immediate needs and opportunities of the moment. The confluent or individuating teacher is that person who by intent, training or experience, can deal effectively with the differences in herself and is sensitive to the differences in her students.

All of us, students and teachers alike, have our own particular orientations toward life and learning. None of these orientations is exactly alike. Each person's orientation must be nurtured and developed to its fullest. Yet no single process is apt to work for persons with different orientations. Jung emphasized that who we are is both genetically and environmentally determined and that our natural orientations cannot and should not be changed or tampered with. Rather, we need to perfect our natural orientations, to distinguish our abilities, and to develop competence and trust in the gifts of attitude and function that are our unique property. At the same time, Jung spoke of the need all of us have to become whole, confluent, and individuated. We have a biological compulsion to be all that we can be. It is this compulsion that provides the mental energy to discover our true selves and to work to fulfill our potential. The need for wholeness also results in the struggle between perfection and completion. This dualism reminds us of one of the profound mysteries of life and learning, that we are only as we become. This mystery is already set upon as the conflict within ourselves between life and death.

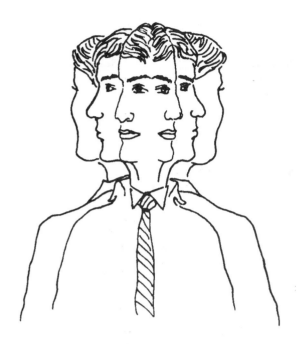

Finally, Jung reminds us that all four functions exist in all of us. They are given to us as potentialities to be developed. As individuals and as teachers, we have a responsibility to develop each of these functions to its fullest. Indeed, the primary role of the school should be that of an exercise ground for becoming confluent and whole as persons.

Utilizing Self-Knowledge in Teaching

The value of the self-insight exercises in this manual and their resultant profiles is to provide the reader with a stepping-off point to better "read" the messages of behavioral diversity in ourselves and our students. This enhanced awareness of who we are and how we function may enable us to take a more objective view of our own motivations and behaviors. Such self-knowledge will, in turn, lead to greater control and freedom over our conscious behaviors. The teacher who understands how she prefers to function and who has terms with which to classify and define these behaviors will be better able to understand, classify, and work with the behaviors of her students.

To achieve this goal of providing opportunities for wholeness for our students (and ourselves), it is recommended that teachers plan and provide for an enriched diversity of learning experiences across the four teaching-learning styles. By providing such a mixture of experiences each day, every student, for at least part of the time, can work toward perfection in his preferred style. The other portions of the day provide him with the experiences and challenges to develop his lesser-used gifts and preferences as steps toward confluence, completion and wholeness.

The teacher's role is to recognize, respect, and use the inborn drives of the learner. Accepting the learner's compulsions to operate in specific ways "validates" his behavior and helps to free him so he will risk behaviors in his less well-developed styles. The more the student is approved for the way in which he prefers to learn, the more he is willing to risk altering those ways! For example, the Intuitive-Thinking learner should not only be provided with opportunities to fully exploit the strengths of the Intuitive-Thinking style, but he should also be encouraged to simultaneously express and appreciate his less-preferred functions of feeling and sensing. By the same token, the extrovert needs to be provided with opportunities to interact, to take action, to discuss ideas, and to work with others. On the other hand, he must also be encouraged to work independently, to become more self-aware, to learn to be more reflective, to appreciate more of his own inner thoughts and feelings, and to commit himself to completing tasks of high personal importance. In short, Jung would say that the primary role of the teacher is to recognize the many potentialities of her students and to consciously plan for the balanced development of each individual across the four styles.

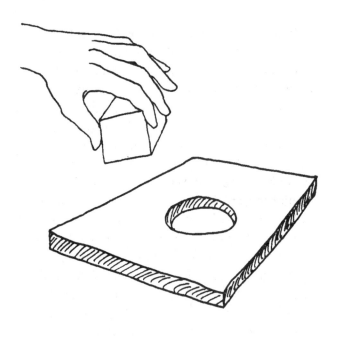

Incompatibility Due to Type

When a student's preferred style is, for whatever reasons, not approved or deemed inappropriate or unacceptable, the student is compelled to assume a set of behaviors often contrary to what fits him personally. This often results in such incompatibilities in the classroom between teacher and pupils that problems become a mainstay of the instructional day. Additionally, when a student is continually required to operate outside of his dominant style, he must compensate in some way for this lack of skills or lack of confluence. This continuing need to compensate, unmatched by any teacher-affirming actions, results in understandably negative reactions. On the other hand, all learning outside of our preferred styles begins by compensating. The teacher must be sensitive to the point at which student frustration replaces interest and commitment. The sensitive teacher can employ both the positive and negative results of compensating behaviors if she is alert to the student's preferred styles of operation. For example, the Intuitive-Feeling student who is disorganized may compensate by making repeated lists of things to do. On the other hand, if there is not some teacher recognition for his efforts, he may become contemptuous of the need for organization and detail, and suffer the consequences of this neglect. "Suffering any consequences," of course, leads to growing incompatibility and less willingness to assume risks.

The Sensing-Feeling student compensates for his need to be personally involved by wanting to help others, by being in group problem-solving situations, and by efforts to talk about the relationship between what is to be learned and his own experiences. The negative side of this compensation may be that he chooses to play the class clown, or that he talks too much, or that he imposes himself on others who don't want his help.

When students are compelled over long periods of time to work in their tertiary or inferior styles, the result is often repeated failure and eventual withdrawal—mental, physical, or both.

In a study undertaken in Florida by Natter and Rollins (1974), 1,500 adults who did not finish the eighth grade were tested using the Myers Briggs Type Indicator. This instrument provides insights into personality type depending on the individual's preferred functions. Of those eighth grade dropouts tested, 99.6% were identified as "sensing dominant." Also tested were 671 finalists for the National Merit Scholarships. Of this number, 83% were "intuitive dominants." The unavoidable lesson to be learned form these findings is that "sensing learners" are penalized in schools and "Intuitives" are affirmed. A corollary lesson is that we need to adopt more activities in the Sensing style if these learners are to be given an opportunity to perfect their type and to grow intellectually. Isabel Briggs Myers reminds us that sensing students focus their interests and attention upon concrete reality that is immediately apparent to one or more of the senses. Thus, Sensing dominant learners are most interested in action, in doing tangible and immediate things. They are not good at listening. They prefer not to deal in abstractions or symbol systems. Their dependence on sense-derived data also gives them an insatiable appetite for activity; any kind of activity is preferable to limited or no activity.

The Intuitive Learner, on the other hand, enjoys working with ideas, possibilities, meanings, relationships, and their consequent symbol systems. Abstractions are turned into words, and words themselves become greater abstractions. Intuitive children, therefore, tend to take an active interest in things school teaches, e.g., language, number combinations, and the statement of various kinds of relationships. They way most schools are now conducted, it is not difficult to see why Sensors fail and Intuitors succeed. Over the course of the last 200 years, school systems have filtered out the Sensing-dominant learners, and only the Intuitives that have survived the system advance to higher levels. To reverse this age-old penchant for conformity teachers must actively plan for and engage all students in all four styles. She must validate them for the style in which they are comfortable and then challenge them to become something more.

The Fifth Function and Neurotic States

We are not alone in this struggle to take control of our psyches. A fifth psychic operation, the transcendent function, is in our minds as a "teacher" to bridge the gaps between the conscious and unconscious, and to guide us to wholeness. But its role needs to be recognized. The transcendent function operates as a biological drive to accelerate our consciousness of all our capacities. The way teachers facilitate this drive toward mental health and wholeness is in providing students with the encouragement they need to see their own unlimited capacities; to become increasingly self-aware, and to learn those skills that will allow them to reach their goals. But, as with inferior functions there is always a flip side. To "deny" the transcendent function's role in self-awareness means that we destabilize ourselves. It's similar to an aircraft that has lost some critical control device and is now plummeting through space in its own random way. A crash is virtually inevitable. The crash takes the form of what society calls neurosis or mental illness. To resist the "whole-making" or

healing actions of the transcendent function is to be out-of-balance, to be disoriented, and to spend most of one's time compensating. The forms of the neurosis are, paradoxically, the exaggerated forms of the dominant functions. Where any set of functions, i.e., a dominant style, has been developed to the virtual exclusion of the other functions, and most particularly, the opposite functions, their imbalance as neurosis appears. To be mentally healthy, then, means to have all functions in some kind of dynamic balance. For teachers to be effective with students this balance must be represented by teaching over each of the style positions, i.e., teaching around the wheel! What are some of the consequences when we don't balance our instruction around the wheel?

For students or adults who are sensing-thinkers (ST's) to the exclusion of the other three positions, i.e., they only concern themselves with order, the objective, precision, facts, sequences, the impersonal, the practical, the measurable; then the preoccupation results in an obsessive-compulsive neurosis. This neurosis, especially and ironically if the ST neurotics are very competent at what they do, disallows them the consciousness to recognize and practice the opposing functions. A neuroses from Jung's point of view is a message from the psyche that tells us of a prior personal wounding, i.e., a severe deprivation (probably experienced in childhood) that has never been acknowledged or filled. The neurosis is the acting-out, unconsciously, of that age-old wound. The neurosis is a voice calling on us to recognize an unfulfilled hunger.

Jung's approach to understanding mental illness and emotional disorientation is to direct us to the underlying need. As such the illness and its symptoms are interpreted as positive indications of the content of a cure. Thus, as earlier noted, the balance needed to counteract any neuroses lies in the exercise of the opposing functions! For the ST obsessive-compulsive the antidote is to practice the intuitive-feeling behaviors! Where the ST earlier insisted on order, precision, sequence, cleanliness, and sterility, the "teacher" now gently guides the learner into the NF capacities to see beauty, richness, multiple alternatives (instead of a correct way), different approaches, aesthetics, color, other feeling states, creative capacity, and a reordering of what's really important based on the psyche's feelings and needs for wholeness.

For very strongly intuitive-thinking (NT) persons the neurosis often takes the form of depression. Depression manifests itself primarily as the absence of good feelings (dysphoria), low self-esteem (often even self-hatred), anger (anything from annoyance to actual hostility), morbidity (thoughts of death), the inability to take pleasure in people, things, or accomplishments (anhedonia), negative self-evaluation (even if their work is done at a very high level), hopelessness, self pity (life seen as unfair), indecisiveness, social withdrawal, fatigue, unusual weight loss or gain, and decreased academic performance.

The degree of the seriousness of the depression involves the number of co-occurring symptoms taking place over prolonged periods of time. But any extended symptomatic behaviors are representations of such a dependency on rational, objective, evidential, analytic, impersonal, inferential and inductive thinking that life has been reduced to formula, to hypotheses, to abstract concepts. The particular dilemma of the NT depressed learner is that there **is** evidence for why it's justifiable to feel (not think) the way they do. Notice, paradoxically, that the illness comes from restricted thinking, but manifests itself, always, as feeling. The inability of the NT student to make distinctions between what they think and how they feel, and their dependency on thinking, to save them from their feelings, intensifies the neurosis. As with obsessive-compulsives the depressive disorders are calls for help. Depressive disorders trace their root causes back to severe deprivation, alienation, exposure to depressed adults, neglect, abuse and/or authoritarian control.

The antidote for the NT lies in the SF position. In the SF position the teacher gently guides the NT depressives into more social

contacts, encourages the expression of feelings, has the student work in cooperative groups, does role plays, builds empathy skills, teaches about learning profiles, has students make their own style/profile portraits (mandalas), read problem-solving stories about students with similar disabilities, tell stories, build friendships, join other student groups, learn to take pleasure from little things, enjoy food, and gripe and complain where there's no possibility of penalty or repercussions, etc.

We've put depression in the NT style because this neurosis is the result of incorrect thinking, i.e., what hurts the student the most is thinking something's so when it's actually not. All styles experience some forms of depression. When the depression is intensified because of thinking then that makes it specifically an NT issue, i.e., the more we try to think our way out of it, the more intense it becomes. For the depressed NT the cure is not in thought but in the taking of direct action. The cure is in acting like an SF!

For the very strong sensing-feeler (SF) the neurosis is hysteria. Males and females are susceptible to hysteria, though it tends to take different forms in each gender. Where the SFs have so developed and relied so exclusively upon their own feelings, their own experience, their dependencies on others for self-identification, e.g., friends, gang members, teams, etc., their personal losses, alienation, low self-esteem, personal rejection (these can be very subtle), loss or absence of recognition, dashed expectations (often unrealistic) and broken dreams can result in loss of self-control, i.e., an hysteric reaction. In heightened cases of loss, the behavior can be destructive toward things, places and other people—where the other person is somehow seen as responsible for the SF's acute disappointment. Hysteric males are more likely to be destructive toward things and people than females. Hysteria in females is often accompanied by self-deprivation (e.g., won't eat; can't sleep), crying, self-accusation, and sometimes self-hatred (though usually for very short periods of time). Hysteria is the quasi-delusional experience of being totally self-dependent with the simultaneous recognition that one is alone and defenseless. The confrontation, on a feeling level, of acute vulnerability results in severe stress. The stress is relieved by acting out the anguish as a manifestation of the complete loss of self-control.

To work with the SF hysterics, the teacher gently guides the student into the NT position, in effect, to ground their thinking in facts and reasonable explanations. In the NT position the SF is supported in suspending feelings until the actual causes of the hysteric breakdown can be identified, analyzed, evaluated and articulated in more meaningful ways. The teacher does not deny any of the hysteric's feelings. The feelings are taken as absolutes. Yes, the student did experience the feelings reported, or, yet, perhaps other feelings still to be reported that might provide greater insight into the anguish. To work with the hysteria as a positive message of the SF's needs, the teacher has the student act like an NT and gathers more information, make connections within the information, relate the intensity of the feelings to prior and similar events, see connections between what triggered this breakdown with prior trauma, and then have the student talk through ways of working with those triggers or emotional messages should they occur again. In effect, the teacher is affirming the students' feelings but modeling the process for recognizing and taking greater control over one's life.

Of all the style-based neuroses, hysteria is probably the easiest to recognize and the least difficult to work with. As with the other neuroses, hysteria is a cry for help. The very nature of the cry gives us clues as to where to look for help.

In all our efforts to help students gain awareness and self-control over their lives, we've become aware of one startling fact. One doesn't change one's behavior through insight! Rather, one changes one's behavior by acting differently. To help children who are imbalanced and destabilized— before things get worse—teachers need to recognize the power and energy of the inferior functions and design instruction so that all students experience the mastering of required content in each of the styles and both of the attitudes.

The intuitive-feeling (NF) student who has so focused on being inventive, creative, "way-out," imaginative, seeing the ills of the world, designing alternative lifestyles, artistic, and creatively alone is in danger of a family of neuroses called dissociation. Dissociation, in its early stages, tends to merge the imagined with the real. In later stages the imagined becomes the real as the two realms change places. In early dissociative disorders, dimensions of the student's life are so painful that the imagined is the more comfortable place to be. In advanced stages the need to be in that place takes the form of daytime dreaming, sometimes hallucinations and generally always a non-responsiveness to one's home and school responsibilities. Dissociation also results in confusion over identity, the exaggeration of one's importance, or obversely, acute feelings of self-negation and unworthiness.

Dissociation is the NF neurosis of choice! Since the creative impulse in the NF comes from their willingness to allow their feelings to interpret their intuitions, the NF is really connected to the energies of the unconscious. That connection is part of the problem. To be involved with the unconscious without first being grounded consciously is to be overwhelmed and decentered. The dissociative disorder is a manifestation of the imbalance.

To work with the NF dissociatives the teacher gently guides the student into the ST position, in effect, bringing the NF back down to the ground to act with the concrete things of life in a more orderly way. Here students are affirmed for their imaginative capacities, but are also encouraged to put things in a more productive order. The dissociative is helped to realize that dreams become reality by hard work, practice, paying attention to the details, looking for the facts, scheduling resources and energies according to what is actually available, and mastering the skills and technique to bring the NF's art to completion.

The NF's dreams must be encouraged and accepted. But by the same token, the purpose of dreams is to bring about change and to produce things of beauty and social value. Working constructively with dissociative disorders means balancing one's teaching behaviors over both possibilities and results. It means affirming the student's needs but simultaneously providing an environment for productivity in the real world with real things.

A Diagnostic and Prescriptive System

As we have repeatedly emphasized, Jung's typology and the Thoughtful Education adaptation of it are not meant to be still another mechanistic or stereotyped way of classifying people. Rather, the model was adapted from Jung's thinking as a way (among many) to think through how one can classify, analyze, and better work with different types of learners. The labels of attitude, function, style, and profile are designed for no other reason than to assist the reader in identifying and working constructively with differences. Thus, even within a single style, within a single attitude, and within the same learning environment, no two persons of the same age and sex will respond in exactly the same way. Since no two of us are alike, it is not surprising that each struggles toward individuation or wholeness in different ways. The teacher, as facilitator of the learning process, must understand that there are many destinations and, simultaneously, many alternative routes to those same destinations. She must also understand that we are all compelled toward wholeness and that in this process, we each need all the help, understanding, and assistance we can get.

Conclusion

These final paragraphs bring us full cycle back to where we began. The able teacher must know herself if she is to be sensitive to her students. She must be able to accept and like herself if she is to be free to accept and like her students. She must feel comfortable with her own nature and learning styles if she is to be able to stimulate her students to search actively for theirs. As a role model for her students, she must enjoy the process of growth and becoming if she is to encourage them to live vigorously, enthusiastically, and without fear. She must, in short, rejoice in her calling, and in her being.

Carl Gustav Jung

A Brief Biography

Carl Gustav Jung was born in 1875 in Kesswil, Switzerland. He was born into a family of Lutheran clergymen, including his father and eight uncles. His mother was the daughter of his father's Hebrew professor.

Jung's father, an extremely well-educated man, began Jung's education in Latin and the classics when Jung was six. Jung himself was raised and trained as a classics scholar which accounts for his later historical-anthropological-archeological approach to the study of man's psyche.

Jung attended the university of Basel. The reading of a selection by a famous neurologist, Krafft-Ebing, pointed Jung toward psychiatry as the field that would allow him to pursue his interests both in medicine and philosophy/anthropology.

Following his graduation, he took a position at the Burgholzi Hospital in Zurich where he served under Eugen Bleuler, the noted psychiatrist who had coined the term schizophrenia. It was at the Burgholzili Hospital (1900-1909) that Jung became recognized as a world authority on mental illness and the constructs of the psyche. During this time Jung coined the term complex in response to his research and experimentation on the word association test, and wrote the first of what was to become the 20-volume collection of published works. Jung's investigations also led to new understanding about personality, e.g., the notions of introversion and extroversion, the function of the archetypes, the role of the libido, and the theories explaining how psychic energy operates.

Jung and Freud worked together for a number of years until theoretical and personal issues led to a break in their professional association.

Jung was an experienced world traveler, having made trips to the United States, Africa, Sudan, Egypt, and India. These trips made him aware of the pervasive images of his classical studies which he eventually identified as universal symbols or archetypes, i.e., the structural elements of the personal and collective unconscious.

After his break with Freud, he underwent a very difficult transitional period (1913-1917) characterized by some inner uncertainty and disorientation. It was also in this period that he underwent his own analysis. From this period emerged his major work on Psychological Types (1921).

By 1936 Jung had been recognized as a scholar of the highest rank. He served as the president of the International Psycho-Analytical Association, was awarded eight honorary degrees, and was made an Honorary Fellow of the Royal Society. He served on the faculties of both the Universities of Zurich and Basel. During these years he saw patients, wrote prolifically, studied the classical texts in Hebrew, Greek, and Latin, and learned enough languages to conduct his medical experiments in many countries. His work and his writings made possible the study of what he later called "analytical psychology." He died in Zurich at his lakeside estate in 1961. His was a life marked by physical vigor, a great openness to life's experiences, a private relationship of warmth and intimacy with his wife and children, and an insatiable hunger for wisdom and understanding.

Notes

Chapter I

[1] Adapted from a workshop experience directed by Dr. Alexis Lotas of Mt. Clements, Michigan, summer, 1977.

[2] Muska Mosston, Teaching: From Comand To Discovery (Belmont, California: Wadsworth Publishing Co., 1972), p. 5.

Chapter II

[1] C.G. Jung, Psychological Types, Bollingen Series XX, Volume 6, The Collected Works (Princeton, N.J.: Princeton University Press, 1971).

[2] Ibid, p. 481.

[3] Isabel Briggs Myers, Manual: Myers Briggs Type Indicator (Palo Alto, CA, Consulting Psychologist Press, 1962, Rev. 1975).

Chapter III

[1] Karen Horney, Self Analysis (New York: W.W. Norton, 1942), pp. 21-22.

[2] Frank Goble, The Third Force: The Psychology of Abraham Maslow (New York: Grossman, 1970), p. 60.

[3] Joseph Luft and Harry Ingram, Group Processes: An Introduction to Group Dynamics (National Press Books), pp. 11-20.

References

Barbe, W. B. & Swassing, R. H. *Teaching through modality strengths: concepts and practice.* Columbus, Ohio: Zaner-Bloser, 1979.

Bloom, Benjamin, (Ed). *Taxonomy of Educational Objectives: Handbook I Cognitive Domain.* New York: David McKay Co., Inc., 1956.

Butler, Kathleen. *Learning and teaching style in theory and practice,* Columbia, CT. The Learner's Dimension, 1984.

Carbo, Marie, and R. and K. Dunn. *Teaching students to read through their individual learning styles.* Englewood Cliffs, NJ: A Reston Book, Prentice Hall, 1986.

Costa, A. *The enabling behaviors, a course syllabus.* San Anselmo, CA: Search Models Unlimited, 1982.

deBono, Edward. *CORT thinking program.* Fairview Park, Elmsford, IL: Pergamon Press, 1975.

Dunn, R. & Dunn, K. *Teaching students through their individual learning styles.* Reston, VA: Reston Publishing Co., (Prentice Hall), 1978.

Fizzell, L. "The Status of Learning Styles," *Educational Forum,* Vol. 48, Spring, 1984. pp. 303-311.

Flavell, J. H. *The developmental psychology of Jean Piaget.* New York: D. Van Nostrand Co., 1963. pp. 85-236.

Gardner, H. *Frames of mind: the theory of multiple intelligences.* New York: Basic Books, 1983.

Gregorc, A. *Learning/teaching styles: their nature and effects, student learning styles: diagnosing and prescribing programs.* Reston, VA: National Association of Secondary School Principals, 1979.

Gregorc, Anthony. *Inside styles: beyond the basics.* Maynard, MA: Gabriel Systems, Inc., 1985.

Guild, P. B. & Garger, S. *Marching to different drummers.* Alexandria, VA: Association for Supervision and Curriculum Development, 1985.

Guilford, J.P. *Way beyond the I.Q.: guide to improving intelligence and creativity.* Buffalo, NY: Creative Energy Foundation, Inc., 1977.

Hanson, J. R. & Silver, H. F. *Teaching Styles And Strategies: Manual #2 in the dealing with diversity series.* Moorestown, NJ: Hanson Silver Strong & Assoc., Inc., 1978, 1986 (2nd ed.)

Hanson, J. R. & Silver, H. F. *Learning Styles And Strategies.* Moorestown, NJ: Hanson Silver Strong & Assoc., Inc., 1978.

Hanson, J. R. *Learning Styles and Visual Literacy. Research Monograph Series #1.* Moorestown, NJ: Hanson Silver Strong & Assoc., Inc., 1987.

Harrison, F. & Bramson, R. M. *The art of thinking.* New York: Berkeley Books, 1982.

Hermann, Ned. "The creative brain," *Training and Development Journal,* July-December, 35, (2), 12-16, 1981.

Holland, J. L. *The self-directed search: professional manual.* Palo Alto, CA: Consulting Psychologist Press, Inc., 1979, pp. 3-5.

Joyce, B. & Weil, M. *Models of teaching.* Englewood Cliffs, NJ: Prentice Hall, 1978.

Jung, Carl G. *Psychological types.* Princeton, NJ: Princeton University Press, 1921.

Keefe, J., (Ed). *Student learning styles: Diagnosing and prescribing programs.* Reston, VA: National Association of Secondary School Principals, 1979.

Keefe, James, (Ed). *Student learning styles and brain behavior*. Reston, VA: National Association of Secondary School Principals, 1982.

Keefe, James. *Learning style: theory and practice*. Reston, VA: National Association of Secondary School Principals, 1987.

Kolb, D. A., Rubin, I. M. & McIntyre, J. M. *Organizational psychology: An experiential approach*. Englewood Cliffs, NJ: Prentice Hall, 1971.

Kolb, D. A. *Experiential learning*. Englewood Cliffs, NJ: Prentice Hall, 1984.

Krathwohl, D. R., Bloom, B. S. & Masia, B. B. *Taxonomy of Educational Objectives: Handbook II Affective Domain*. New York: David McKay Co., Inc., 1956.

Lawrence, G. *People types and tiger stripes: A practical guide to learning styles*. Gainesville, FL: Center for Applications of Psychological Type, Inc., 1979.

Lowen, Walter. *Dichotomies of the mind*. New York: John Wiley & Sons, 1982.

McCarthy, B. *The 4MAT system*. Arlington Heights, IL: Excell Publishing Co., 1982.

McCaulley, M. H. *"The Myers Briggs Type Indicator and the teaching learning process,"* a paper presented @ AERA, 1974, Chicago, and available through CAPT, Gainesville, FL, 1976.

Meeker, Mary. SOI Systems, Box D, Vida, Oregon.

Myers, I. B. *Manual: The Myers-Briggs type indicator*. Palo Alto, CA: Consulting Psychologists Press, 1962, 1975.

Myers, I. & Myers, P. *Gifts differing*. Palo Alto, CA: Consulting Psychologists Press, 1980.

Riso, Don. *Personality types*. Boston, MA: Houghton Mifflin Co., 1987.

Singer, June & Loomis, Mary. *Inventory of Personality*. Detroit, MI: Wayne State University, Center for the Study of Cognitive Processes, 1979.

Witkin, H. *Cognitive style and the teaching-learning process*. AERA audiotape, 1974.

Appendices

Appendix A

A Comparative Analysis of Learning Style Models

Dr. J. Robert Hanson

1996

Learning style models are myriad. By different names such categorization procedures have been applied since 1000 BC. But when a school or district adopts a model and budgets the resources to implement its procedures, the model needs to be responsive to the following criteria. In effect, a good and workable classroom model must account behaviorally for:

1. All types of learners—not just those who do well in school.

2. All types of content—not just recall or reasoning objectives.

3. All kinds of assessment—not just true/false or fill in the blanks.

4. All kinds of intelligences—not just logical-mathematic, spatial and linguistic.

5. All kinds of cultural variations—not just white Anglo-Saxon.

In addition, the model must account for:

6. A concept of intellectual and emotional wholeness—not just the age dependence on cognition.

7. Intervention processes that provide for the constructive use of differences in instruction and assessment.

8. A reproducible methodology, i.e., is the model theoretically sound, comprehensive, reflective of prior research, and will its developmental procedures result in the same outcomes when tried in your schools and classes?

9. The inclusion and interpretation of all other models, modalities, cultural variations and intelligences.

10. Diagnostic and prescriptive features.

11. Explanations of how the mind works, psychic motivation, and mental disorders.

12. Simplicity of use—can classroom teachers implement these procedures in their classes?

Models tend to fall into five categories:

1. Jungian-based models include Myers (1962) and McCaulley (1974), Hanson and Silver (1978), Gordon Lawrence (1979), David Kiersey (1978), Michael Malone (11977), Alexis Lotas (1977), Simon and Bryan (1977), Walter Lowen (1982), Arraj and Arraj (1985) and Keith Golay (1982). These models are specifically focused on Jung's theories about the oppositional nature of the functions and the polarities that identify, in different combinations, discrete types, whether on three dimensions (Jung), four dimensions (Myers) or more (Lowen).

2. Experiential and observationally derived models include Kurt Lewin (1935), David Kolb (1971), Bernice McCarthy (1980), Anthony Gregorc (1982), David Hunt (1987), Kathleen Butler (1984) and Don Riso (1987). These models specifically reflect a cognitive orientation both in terms of the selection of research populations and various, though very eclectic, developmental methodologies.

3. Cognitive models or categorical systems include Joyce-Weil (1978), John Holland (1979), Harrison and Bramson (1982), Joe Hill (1971), J.P. Guilford (1977) and Mary Meeker. These programs have a distinctly cognitive orientation focused on the so-called "higher order" thought processes. These models tend to be very descriptive of different kinds of strategies or behaviors, but tend not

to operate from larger theoretical models. The methodology is one of making inferences about specific types of school-related tasks or curriculum objectives and classifying these types based on recurring similarities of function or purpose.

4. Pattern-derived programs are a subset of cognitive models but are not sets of polarities. They include Dunn and Dunn (1975), Keefe (1982), Letteri (1987) and Carbo (1985). These programs have extensive diagnostic and prescriptive insights and work well for increasing achievement in the lower and higher order cognitive areas. They do not represent larger theoretical constructs about style, nor do they address the intrapsychic issues of motivation, psychic energy, or mental and emotional wholeness.

5. Brain/mind models include the works of Ned Hermann (1981), Bandler and Grinder (1979) and Eyesenck (1965), among others. These models identify aspects of brain physiology or function localization. Research in this area tends to be restricted to descriptive tasks of the brain, not mind, and is still in search of a unifying hypothesis(ses). To date, brain-based models should be understood as preliminary and exploratory, and not as a theoretical basis for model-making.

Exemplary Learning Style Models

Building an exemplary learning-styles program need not be difficult. There are, however, necessary precautions. Of the five schools of models, single models stand out as representative of the best that a particular school has to offer, and that should be considered as the foundation or starting place for a more comprehensive program. Planning should be undertaken as a multiple year process and developed systematically, component by component. For example, most of the better theoretical models do not include intervention strategies, e.g., Myers, Lowen, Kolb, or the single construct theorists. Few models include instrumentation for the traditional modalities, as well as the newer dimensions. Assessment instrumentation varies from acceptable to

downright careless. Most of the school-based models don't suggest a picture of wholeness, or deal with psychological drives, e.g., motivation, defenses, forms of resistance, etc. With these precautions in mind, our recommendation for starting places, by schools, are as follows:

1. Of the Jungian-based models, (the largest of the schools in terms of modifications and certainly the best researched of all the schools), the most distinguished theoretical treatments are Lowen's (1982) and Myers (1962), and the most practical applications are those of Hanson and Silver (1987). Most of the long term research has been done by the Myers Briggs Type Indicator community at their Florida center in Gainesville, and/or as reported by the Journal of Psychological Type out of Mississippi State University.

2. Of the experiential school the most distinguished theoretical treatment is David Kolb's "An Experiential Approach" (1974). The most practical application of Kolb's model is Bernice McCarthy's 4 MAT system (1982).

3. Of the cognitive models important theoretical work has been done, under different headings by Costa (1982), Bloom (1956), Guilford (1968), deBono (1975), Gardner (1983) and others. Practical classroom applications are Marzano's "Tactics for Thinking" (1986), and Mary Meekers's SOI. The publications of Anita Harnadeck and Sandra Black (Midwest Publications, Palo Alto, CA, Arthur Whimbey (1980), Richard Paul, Richard Samson (1965) and a host of others, fill the necessary gaps.

4. Of the pattern-derived programs the theoretical work has been done by many different researchers. Maximum usage of different single construct variables, in different combinations, has been effectively implemented by Dunn and Dunn (1978) and Carbo (1985).

5. Of the modalities or perception functions there is an enormous body of theoretical material, some instrumentation, but sadly very little has been written in terms of teacher intervention techniques to improve the skills

of perception. Barbe and Swassing (1979) is a good place to begin for assessments of student modality strengths.

6. Of the brain-derived models there is a growing body of theoretical literature but little of immediate practical consequence for classroom intervention. This developing research needs to be carefully monitored and evaluated, and very cautiously adopted. Howard Gardner's multiple intelligences work has become popular (1983).

Assessing the Theoretical Models

For a model to be used as the basis of a comprehensive learning program, and where the model itself may have components missing, other models can be adopted and/or modified. Most of the models currently in circulation are troubled, based on our criteria, by the following deficiencies:

1. The models were hypothesized against the demands of a primarily cognitive curriculum and hence tend to overlook, or to have underdeveloped, the feeling positions, most particularly the creative/innovative intuitive-feeling position, e.g. Bruce Joyce's (1978) categorization of teaching models doesn't even list this style as a category. Gregorc's model (1982), as a rational problem-solving model, has neither perceptual functions nor well developed descriptions of the creative and imagistic learner. Kolb (1971) and Riso's (1987) models, essentially rationally-focused problem-solving models, have no well developed intuitive-feeling descriptions. More recently Keefe's (1987) work, essentially a cognitively-focused set of single construct variables, specifically omits the roles of affect in learning styles. The role of affect or feeling in learning is critical to gaining and securing attention, to retention and to having students assume ever larger responsibilities for their own learning. To be aware of one's own feeling states and to be able to identify and articulate those states, is the highest form of rationality.

Such sensitivities stand as the gate-keepers to intellectual maturity and to independence of thought. To adopt learning style models that do not include descriptions of the roles of affect in learning is tantamount to asking students to remember bodies of information without ever simultaneously asking them to make decisions about meaning or applicability.

2. The models were developed on a too narrowly focused set of learning style dimensions, e.g. omitting the dimension of attitude, or orientation to the world, e.g. as psychic energy sources, often meant that these same forces show up elsewhere but are now disguised as negative emotional drives. Gregorc (1982), for example, indiscriminately mixes the functions of introversion and extraversion in his descriptions of styles. Holland (1979) pulls out introversion and extraversion and uses them as separate and distinct styles in themselves, along with four other separate and distinct styles. The cognitive theorists don't include the psychic energy drives at all, letting their models stand, rather, as static behavioral descriptions.

3. The models emerged from an evolutional process based on recurring observed behaviors rather than on a more methodological approach combining systems theory considerations with a thorough knowledge of theories of personality. Observational systems work very well when all the variables to be systematized are represented in the observed population. Again, we don't tend to find what we don't believe is present. The models which tend to be most inclusive, therefore, are the models emerging from personality theory, and not from cognition, or school settings, or steps in problem-solving.

4. The models have emerged, understandably, in this early developmental process as essentially static descriptions of the different styles. One looks in vain in the educational literature for discussions of motivational triggers, or descriptions of the styles as a result of dependencies on a particular

perceptual function triggering a judgment function, etc. In light of the very short history of learning styles a next major developmental push must be to identify how the particular styles actually function by describing the interactions that occur. Walter Lowen's work (1982) and the works of Jung and some his interpreters, provide insights for this next phase of learning style descriptions in their dynamic forms.

It is fascinating to note that learning styles modeling is a phenomenon in education of just the last 20 years. A quick review of the literature indicated that 95% of the educational models are titles published since 1978. Each successive year has brought with it improved models and better attempts at instrumentation. There is reason to be optimistic about future developments if a cooperative and dialectical process can be put in place and maintained.

5. The models were developed without a concept of intellectual or emotional wholeness. Some of the models, e.g., Keefe (1982), Harrison-Bramson (1982), Kolb (1971), allow themselves to be seduced by the idea that learning is primarily information-processing, i.e., the so-called higher level cognitive functions, e.g., analysis, inference, evaluation, etc. Other models propose that styles of learners be matched to styles of teaching, e.g. Dunn and Dunn (1978) , Golay (1982). Matching learning style with teaching style is essential for the purposes of affirming the student's learning style strengths, and for increasing recall capacities. To teach to the student's potential for wholeness, however, means that the teacher must not only affirm the student in his/her own style, but also challenge them to develop their more latent capacities by working with content in the other style areas as well. Success in the student's areas of learning style strength is the psychological or motivational trigger to being willing to work on a more foreign soil.

6. Finally, the models need accompanying instrumentation that not only reflects all the basic learning styles, and that results in profiles of strengths and liabilities for each of the styles, but that also provide for responses that are not forced choice, either/or, type categories. Since learning style instrumentation, by definition, will remain in the "self-report" category, instrument designers, perhaps following the examples of Singer and Loomis (1979), can vastly improve the self-report process by allowing greater respondent choice in assigning weights to those items that are perceived as preferences, even though, theoretically, the two choices may be oppositional in nature.

The models that follow are evaluated against the following 10 criteria:

1. addresses all styles of learners

2. addresses ways to categorize all forms of content

3. includes diagnostic, prescriptive and optimization procedures

4. contains wholeness concept

5. includes intervention processes to maximize all kinds of capacities, e.g. teaching strategies

6. contains a reproducible methodology

7. contains valid instrumentation

8. explains motivation by styles

9. is consistent with systems theory

10. includes an explanation for how the mind works

A COMPARATIVE ANALYSIS OF LEARNING STYLE MODELS

Code: P = present;   A = absent;   PM = present but certain styles missing

Models' criteria	1	2	3	4	5	6	7	8	9	10
Bloom, B.	PM	PM	A	A	PM	A	A	A	A	A
Butler, K.	PM	PM	PM	P	P	P	A	P	A	A
Dunn & Dunn	PM	A	P	A	A	A	A	A	A	A
Gardner, H.	P	A	A	P	A	A	A	A	P	P
Gregorc, A.	PM	PM	A	P	P	PM	A	P	A	A
Hanson-Silver	P	P	P	P	P	P	P	P	P	P
Harrison & Bramson	PM	PM	A	A	A	PM	A	A	A	A
Jung, C.G.	P	A	A	P	P	P	A	P	P	P
Keefe, J.	PM	PM	A	A	A	PM	A	A	A	A
Kolb, D.	PM	PM	A	P	P	P	P	P	P	A
McCarthy, B.	PM	PM	P	P	P	P	P	P	P	A
Myers, I.	P	A	P	P	P	P	P	P	P	P
Sternberg, R.	A	A	A	A	A	A	A	A	A	A

Needed Directions

H. L. Mencken once observed that "...for every deep and complex problem there is a single solution, ...and it's always wrong." So what, then, is really needed? As a set of propositions for our ensuing debate I propose the following:

First, the identification and adoption of a set of principles about the architecture of the mind. Carl Jung's theories are a good starting place. His disciples' works deserve serious reading by educators, e.g., Maria Louise VanFranz (1979), Daryl Sharp (1986), Isabel Myers (1962, 1980), Mary McCaulley (1976, 1981), Gordon Lawrence (1979) and Hanson Silver Strong (1978, 1984, 1986), and Hanson (1987, 1988).

Second, the identification and adoption of a set of principles about the nature of intellectual growth and change, i.e., that it is circular, uneven, repetitive, rational and non-rational, inextricably bound to affect and body awareness, and process-focused.

Third, the identification and adoption of teaching strategies for addressing developmental skills in seeing, hearing, speaking, and for the kinesthetic and tactual skills.

Fourth, the identification and adoption of principles and strategies for working more effectively with our feeling-dominant learners. How, for example, are teachers to be trained to deal more effectively with their own emotional states so that they, in turn, can work more constructively with the emotional needs of their students? How, for example, can we build into our basic skills programs the motivation to learn that comes from reading and understanding fairy tales (the windows to the unconscious), or the great myths (the stories of the collective consciousness)?

The identification and adoption of a set of principles that would constitute an education of, and for, the whole child, mind, spirit, affect and physical wellness, and, finally, the identification and mastery of a set of teaching, questioning, coaching, metacognitive, and administrative strategies that will assist teachers and administrators in more fully addressing their own personal and professional goals as self-aware and humane learners and teachers.

Appendix B

A Factor Analytic Study of the Learning Preference Inventory, Based on C. G. Jung's Psychological Types Theory

J. Robert Hanson, Ed.D., Harvey F. Silver, Ed.D., Steven P. Gulkus, Ph.D.

1984

Papers presented at the Annual Meeting of the American Educational Research Association, New Orleans, LA 1984.

The present study tests the use of Jungian based psychological types classification (model) as a means of assessing elementary school aged learner's learning styles. To test this model, a Learning Preference Inventory was constructed from the characteristics Jung (1921) attributes to the six learner types and the two information processing (attitude) functions, and from the Myers-Briggs Type Indicator (1962). The present investigation involves a factor analysis of the items in the Learning Preference Inventory developed by Hanson and Silver (1980).

Method

Subjects

The subject pool consisted of an initial sample of 600 third, fourth, fifth and sixth grade students from South Brunswick Township, New Jersey, a largely urban school district. This sample received the first of the experimental version of the instrument. A second sample of 250 third, fourth, fifth and sixth grade students from the Catskill Public School Systems, a district that contains a mix of urban, suburban, and rural inhabitants. This second sample received the final version; the time-analyzed and rewritten version of the instrument.

Instrument

The tested instrument, the Learning Preference Inventory (LPI), is based on Jung's typological theories, the behavioral definitions of the Myers-Brigs Type Indicator—MBTI (Myers-Briggs, 1962, 1976) and the developers observations of student behaviors (1976-1980). The learning style behaviors, i.e., the pairings of perception and judgment functions, were described as a result of the authors' own observations of over a thousand students in learning situations, as well as conducting teacher training in the use of the model. In these in-service teacher training situations the authors would propose specific student learning behaviors according to the variables of approach to learning, approach to problem-solving, assets and liabilities, and "learns best" behaviors. The teachers would then be invited to provide feedback on their own observations of student behavior. These feedback sessions, the authors' own analysis of the Jungian and Myers-Briggs behaviors, and a thorough study of the literature in the field, resulted in the descriptions of behavior. An instrument was developed that presented the behavioral descriptors in the context of classroom situations.

The actual instrument asked respondents to rank four sets of responses to a single sentence stem. In responding to these questions the subjects rank ordered their preferred responses. Each of the item stems were written in the context of a classroom activity, the four sets of responses for each stem represents student behaviors in response to these activities. For example, "I like assignments or activities which involve 1. taking ideas and changing them into something new and different; 2. searching for solutions to problems; 3. copying or making things; 4. sharing my feelings and ideas." Students were asked to rank the four activities from their most preferred (rank of 1) to their least preferred activity (rank of 4). Each of four responses were designed to represent a pairing of a perception and judgment function. For example, in the latter sample item, response #1 is an intuitive-feeling (NF) preference item; #2 is an intuitive-thinking (NT) preference item; #3 is a sensing-thinking (ST) preference item; and #4 is a sensing-feeling (SF) preference item. Since the information-processing (attitude) functions of introversion and extroversion according to Jung (1921) are used to modify the perception and judgment functions, separate items were written to assess this learner characteristic. The following is an introversion/extroversion item: "In a group I am usually... 1) quiet; 2) noisy; 3) talkative; 4) listening." Responses 1 and 4 are introversion (I) responses 2 and 3 are extroversion (E) responses. Again, students were asked to rank these responses. Item stems as well as their accompanying four responses were randomly positioned in the instrument. The developers of the Learning Preference Inventory along with elementary school teachers developed the items representing learning preferred activities. The initial item pool of 500 items was reduced by testing 600 third, fourth, fifth and sixth grade students and by deleting items that were judged obscure, unclear, or irrelevant. Items were analyzed for clarity, readability, and the degree to which the items represented the typological descriptors proposed by Myers-Briggs (1962-1972). The remaining pool of 35 item stems and the 140 item responses were chosen for the final version of the Learning Preference Inventory. This final version of the LPI contained 25 item stems accompanied by their 4 respective item choices representing behavioral descriptors of the ST, NT, NF and SF learners. The remaining 10 items measured the introversion/extroversion function.

Procedure

A series of warm-up activities were standardized to acquaint the students with self-assessment ranking procedures and the concept of preference. A description of these warm-up activities is presented in Table 1.

TABLE 1
Description of Warm-Up Activities

Before administering the Learning Preference Inventory (LPI) the students need to be reminded that the LPI is not a test since there are no right or wrong answers. It is important to help your students understand the concept of "preference."

Some suggestions for introducing the notion of "preference" to younger students include:
1. Explaining that a preference is a choice between two or more alternatives and the LPI helps us find what we like most to do from the choices presented.

2. As an exercise have the students write down their four favorite TV programs. Have them pretend that all four programs are aired at exactly the same time. Then have them choose which programs they would watch in a first, second, third and last order. Ask them to explain how they made their decision.

3. You may also want to remind the students that choices are not always made from among those things one likes. Sometimes the available choices are equally unlikable: "Which would you rather do—wash dishes or clean your room?" Or, "Would you rather write an essay or take a test?"

These warm-up activities are quite important since many students are so unsure of themselves that self-assessment instruments tend to reflect what the student believes is desired rather than what it is they actually like or want to do.

Teachers practiced the warm-up activities before they actually tested the subjects. In addition, standardized directions were given to the subjects on how to complete the LPI (see Table 2).

TABLE 2
Directions to Subjects

Introduction:
The question you will answer will help us learn more about you, and to help you and your teacher understand more about how you learn. This is not a test. Try to answer as you really prefer to behave. There are no right or wrong answers. All questions must be answered. If you don't understand a word or phrase feel free to ask for help. You have as much time as you need to complete the questions. It's important not to feel rushed.

Directions For Responding:
Each question has four choices. For each of the choices rank order the four choices according to your fist, second, third, and fourth choices. Mark you first choice with a 1, your second choice with a 2, you third with a 3, and your last choice with a 4. See the example below:

    1.   I prefer to learn something new by
        1. (3)   reading a book   (third choice)
        2. (1)   watching a movie   (first choice)
        3. (4)   making a project   (fourth choice)
        4. (2)   working with a friend (second choice)

Make all your responses in the boxes provided.

The most important thing to remember is to take each answer according to how you feel, not how you think you ought to feel. Make your own choices based on your best judgment.

Results

The 144 items were analyzed and intercorrelations were obtained and the resulting matrix was factor analyzed. Analysis of the final version of the LPI generated a 144 x 144 matrix of inter-item correlations as input for the analysis. Prior estimates of communalities and eigenvalues (the characteristic roots of the correlation matrix) adjusted for prior estimates of communalities were included in the analysis. Initial factor loading were generated. Varimax rotations determined the final factor loadings (Harman, 1960).

Items representing each factor were retained if they loaded at least .40 on that factor and if they loaded higher on that factor than on any other. Separate analyses were performed on the 100 perception and judgment items (each of the 25 question stems were accompanied by 4 items representing the combined perception/ judgment behavioral descriptors) and the 40 introversion/extroversion items (10 question stems with 4 items representing 2 introversion and 2 extroversion behavioral descriptors).

The retained factors of the combined perception and judgment functions analysis accounted for 70.31% of the original total variance. Four factors were retained with the following variances accounted for: factor 1—23.50%; factor 2—15.63%; factor 3—16.28%; factor 4—14.90%. Factor 1 loaded on items hypothesized as representing the sensing/feeling (SF) items, factor 2, the sensing/thinking (ST) items; factor 3, the intuitive/feeling (SF) items; and factor 4, the intuitive/thinking (NT) items. In a separate factor analysis applied to the introversion/extroversion items only, the two retained factors accounted for 71.28% of the original total variance: factor 1—35.79% and factor 2—35.49%. Factor 1 corresponds with items hypothesized as representing extroversion (E) items and factor 2 with items hypothesized as representing introversion (I) items. A complete description of the items associated with each factor and their factor loadings is presented in Table 3 for the 100 items representing the combined judgment and perception functions—SF, ST, NF, and NT.

TABLE 3
Factor Structure For The Combined Judgment and Perception Functions: Sensing/Feeling (SF), Sensing/Thinking (ST), Intuitive/Feeling (NF), and Intuitive/Thinking (NT)

Stem and Item Choices	Factor	Loading
1. I'm good at		
1. helping others (SF)	SF	**.64b**
2. getting things done (ST)	NF	**.59**
3. organizing things (NT)	N	**.49**
4. discovering things (NF)	ST	**.47**
2. I like questions that ask me		
1. how I feel about things (SF)	SF	**.58**
2. to choose the correct answer (ST)	ST	**.57**
3. to think of new and original ideas (NF)	NF	**.54**
4. to explain why things happen (NT)	NT	**.52**
3. When I'm making something I prefer to		
1. have someone show me how to do it (SF)	SF	**.64**
2. follow the directions one step at a time (ST)	ST	**.57**
3. figure out how to do it by myself (NT)	NT	**.55**
4. find a new way for doing (NF)	NF	**.44**

continued on next page

continued from previous page

Stem and Item Choices	Factor	Loading

4. I would like to be in
   1. music, painting or writing (NF) — NF — **.61**
   2. science, math or law (NT) — NT — **.47**
   3. business, politics or construction (ST) — ST — **.42**
   4. sales, social work or nursing (SF) — SF — **.41**

5. I work best when
   1. I'm having fun (SF) — SF — **.62**
   2. I know exactly what I have to do (ST) — ST — **.60**
   3. I can choose what I want to learn (SF) — NF — **.55**
   4. I'm finding a solution to a problem (NT) — NT — **.52**

6. I like assignments or activities which involve
   1. sharing my feelings and ideas (SF) — SF — **.65**
   2. searching for solutions to problems (NT) — NT — **.55**
   3. taking ideas and changing them into
      something new and different (NF) — NF — **.50**
   4. copying or making things (ST) — ST — **.42**

7. When I have a difficult assignment I like to
   1. talk with others to see what needs to be done — SF — **.67**
   2. memorize or practice what needs to be done — ST — **.61**
   3. think things through for myself before
      someone explains it to me (NT) — NT — **.52**
   4. find new or different ways of doing
      the assignment (NF) — NF — **.43**

8. I enjoy
   1. doing things I've never done before (NF) — NF — **.68**
   2. working with friends (SF) — SF — **.65**
   3. doing things I know about and can do well (ST) — ST — **.51**
   4. reading about things that interest me (NT) — NT — .37

9. I prefer games that
   1. make me think ahead about what to do
      (chess, Stratego, etc.) (NT) — NT — **.60**
   2. are fast, have a lot of action, and
      where someone wins (ST) — ST — **.50**
   3. everyone can play and where no one loses (SF) — SF — **.47**
   4. I can make up myself (NF) — NF — .40

10. I would like to
    1. help other people (SF) — SF — **.66**
    2. make a lot of money (ST) — ST — **.61**
    3. invent of discover something (NT) — NT — **.54**
    4. create art, music and dance (NF) — NF — **.51**

11. People who know me well would say I'm mostly
    1. caring, friendly and helpful (SF) — SF — **.72**
    2. creative, enthusiastic and imaginative (NF) — NF — **.55**
    3. accurate, hardworking and organized (ST) — NTc — **.47**
    4. logical, sensible and intelligent (NT) — NT — **.43**

continued on next page

continued from previous page

Stem and Item Choices	Factor	Loading
12. In school the most important thing to me is		
1. making friends (SF)	SF	**.71**
2. getting good grades (ST)	ST	**.65**
3. learning how to think and reason for myself (NT)	NT	**.47**
4. using my ideas and imagination (SF)	SFc	**.43**
13. I like to learn about		
1. myself and other people (SF)	SF	**.73**
2. important ideas and why things happen (NT)	NT	**.65**
3. things I can do and use (ST)	ST	**.63**
4. what life may be like in the future (NF)	NF	**.59**
14. I would like a job that allows me to		
1. read and think (NT)	NT	**.63**
2. make things (ST)	NFc	**.59**
3. do unusual things (NF)	NF	**.57**
4. work with people (SF)	SF	**.52**
15. When I have a problem I like to		
1. carefully figure out what needs to be done to solve the problem (NT)	STc	**.60**
2. use a solution I already know about (ST)	NTc	**.45**
3. choose the solution that feels best (SF)	NF	.39
4. think up new and unusual ways to solve it (NF)	NF	.37
16. When I have many assignments to do I		
1. start working right away and finish one assignment before starting another (ST)	ST	**.74**
2. take time to talk with others and check my answers while I work (SF)	SF	**.67**
3. think carefully about what needs to be done, then play how best to do it (NT)	NT	**.60**
4. jump from one assignment to another in no particular order (NF)	NF	.35
17. I like books about		
1. mysteries, science and stories that explain why things happen (NT)	NT	**.67**
2. legends, fantasies, and other people's beliefs (NF)	NF	**.65**
3. people's feelings and personal problems (SF)	SF	**.58**
4. real people (biographies), adventure stories, and how to make things happen (ST)	ST	**.49**
18. I like assignments that		
1. are new and different (NF)	NF	**.68**
2. I know and can do well (ST)	ST	**.65**
3. having people working together helping each other (SF)	SF	**.61**
4. make me think (NT)	NT	**.46**
19. I am at my best when		
1. working in a group (SF)	SF	**.68**
2. finding information and thinking (NT)	NT	**.59**
3. remembering things (ST)	NTc	**.54**
4. coming up with new ideas (NF)	NF	.37

continued on next page

continued from previous page

Stem and Item Choices	Factor	Loading
20. I like to		
1. hear what other people have to say about themselves or about me (SF)	SF	**.73**
2. make something that I can use (ST)	ST	**.63**
3. investigate ideas (NT)	NT	**.59**
4. use my imagination (NF)	NF	**.57**
21. My best ideas come from		
1. talking with people (SF)	SF	**.67**
2. reading about things (NT)	NT	**.57**
3. doing things (ST)	ST	**.54**
4. imagining things (NF)	NF	**.49**
22. I prefer teachers who		
1. want to be my friend (SF)	SF	**.74**
2. teach me how to do useful things (ST)	ST	**.67**
3. encourage me to be creative (NF)	NF	**.50**
4. make me think (NT)	NT	**.45**
23. I prefer assignments		
1. I can do quickly and well (ST)	ST	**.65**
2. allow me to express my feelings and use my imagination (NF)	NF	**.64**
3. have people working to help each other (SF)	SF	**.62**
4. make me think, and may take a long time (NT)	NT	**.54**
24. I prefer to learn by		
1. answering questions in a workbook or on worksheets (ST)	ST	**.60**
2. reading and discovering things for myself (NT)	NT	**.58**
3. doing an original project (NF)	NF	**.56**
4. playing a game (SF)	SF	**.54**
25. I learn best when I can		
1. share my ideas with others (SF)	SF	**.65**
2. look things up and compare ideas (NT)	NT	**.61**
3. do projects of my own choosing (NF)	NF	**.59**
4. apply skills I've already learned or memorized (ST)	ST	**.57**

a Learning style hypothesized for each questions:
ST = Sensing/Thinking, SF = Sensing/Feeling,
NF = Intuitive/Feeling, and NT = Intuitive/Thinking

b Values above .40 are bolded

c Items not matching hypothesized styles

Six items were deleted on the basis of the principal component analysis and seven items did not match the hypothesized styles but loaded on one of the other styles factors. The remaining 94 items were retained to form the four factors.

The introversion and extroversion factors are presented in Table 4. Two items were deleted on the basis of the principal component analysis and only one item did not match the hypothesized I/E prediction. The remaining 38 items loaded either as an extroversion or introversion item.

TABLE 4
Factor Structure For the Information Processing Function: Introversion (I) and Extroversion (E)

Stem and Item Choices	Factor	Loading
1. In a group I am usually		
1. noisy (E)a	E	.72b
2. talkative (E)	E	.68
3. quiet (I)	I	.65
4. listening (I)	I	.61
2. As a person I tend to		
1. talk easily about my feelings and ideas (E)	E	.73
2. keep my thoughts/feelings to myself (I)	I	.69
3. be easy to get to know (E)	E	.64
4. be hard to get to know (I)	I	.43
3. When I'm working I tend to		
1. work with something that takes a long time (I)	I	.59
2. do things quickly (E)	E	.38
3. be carefully (I)	I	.36
4. be impatient with work that takes a long time (E)	E	.33
4. I like		
1. noisy and crowded places where lots of things are happening (E)	E	.71
2. doing lots of different things at the same time (E)	E	.69
3. doing one thing at a time	I	.59
4. quiet places where I can think (I)	I	.46
5. When working on an assignment I prefer working		
1. by myself (I)	I	.66
2. in a quiet place (I)	I	.50
3. in a group with other people (E)	E	.43
4. in a place where I can talk and share with other people (E)	E	.36
6. When I meet new people I		
1. feel comfortable and talk easily (E)	E	.72
2. feel uncomfortable talking with people I don't know (I)	I	.70
3. enjoy talking about myself (E)	E	.67
4. find it difficult to think of good things to say (I)	I	.62

continued on next page

continued from previous page

Stem and Item Choices	Factor	Loading
7. When I feel upset I		
1. keep my feelings to myself (I)	I	**.72**
2. share my feelings to myself (E)	E	**.65**
3. usually let everybody know how I feel (E)	E	**.62**
4. have difficulty telling others how I really feel (I)	I	**.57**
8. In group activities I		
1. listen to what others have to say before I speak (I)	I	**.74**
2. keep my ideas to myself until I'm asked to speak (I)	I	**.69**
3. share my own ideas first and then get reactions (E)	E	**.56**
4. talk a great deal (E)	E	**.54**
9. I really enjoy		
1. talking (E)	E	**.64**
2. reading and thinking (I)	I	**.60**
3. being with people (E)	E	**.60**
4. writing (I)	I	.39
10. When I'm working I prefer to		
1. do one thing carefully before beginning another (I)	I	**.63**
2. do many things at the same time (E)	E	**.59**
3. think a lot before starting (I)	I	**.58**
4. start right away and think about what I'm doing as I go along (E)	E	**.48**

a   Information processing functions hypothesized for each question:
I = Introversion and E = Extroversion

b   Values above .40 are bolded

c   Items not matching hypothesized styles

Both Tables 3 and 4 present the question stem with the four choices associated with the typological characteristics and its associated factor loadings.

Discussion

The present study tested the Jungian psychological type model as a conceptualization of learning styles. There is fairly strong evidence that the Learning Preference Inventory developed by Hanson and Silver (1980) adequately assesses the learner types defined by both Jung (1921) and the Myers-Briggs Type Indicator (Myers-Briggs, 1962, 1976). The factors correspond to those defined by both of these models. The correspondence of the items to the factors that emerged with the hypothesized styles is strikingly consistent across all factors. Only a few items did not load highly enough to be included in any of the six factors tested and only a few items appear to be misplaced in the model. Students perceptions of their own learning styles do appear to be grouped in the manner in which Jung (1921) and Myers-Briggs (1962, 1976) indicated.

Appendix C
Hanson-Silver Learning Preference Inventory

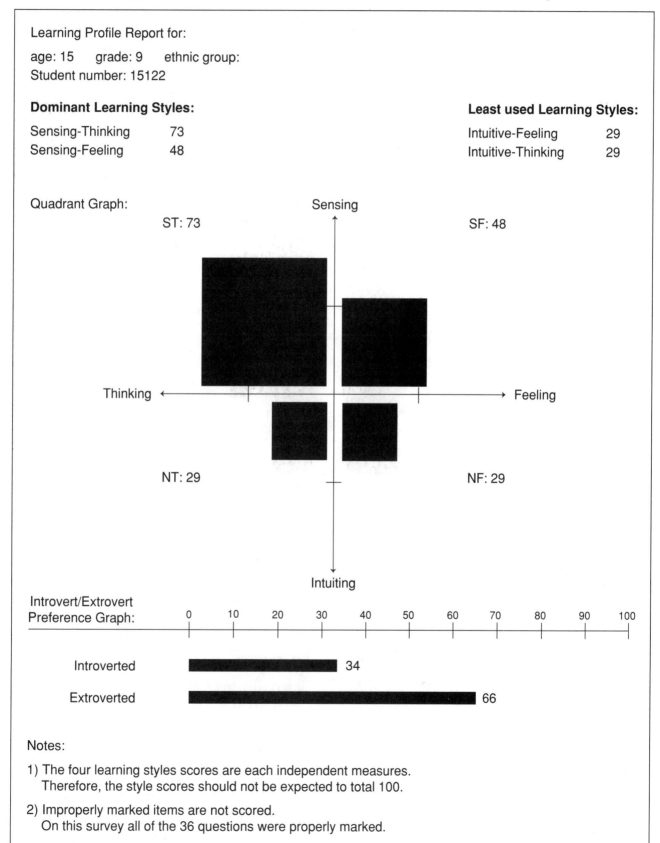

Learning Profile Report for:

age: 15   grade: 9   ethnic group:
Student number: 15122

Dominant Learning Styles:

Sensing-Thinking   73
Sensing-Feeling   48

Least used Learning Styles:

Intuitive-Feeling   29
Intuitive-Thinking   29

Quadrant Graph:

Sensing

ST: 73   SF: 48

Thinking   Feeling

NT: 29   NF: 29

Intuiting

Introvert/Extrovert
Preference Graph:

0 10 20 30 40 50 60 70 80 90 100

Introverted   34

Extroverted   66

Notes:

1) The four learning styles scores are each independent measures.
   Therefore, the style scores should not be expected to total 100.

2) Improperly marked items are not scored.
   On this survey all of the 36 questions were properly marked.

Assets and Liabilities of the Sensing Thinking Learner (ST)

The ST strengths are in his ability to apply himself to the task at hand. He is concerned with action and tangible results. He is highly task-oriented and a good person to have on a committee concerned about getting working done. He is organized, adept at collecting the facts and pays attention to detail. He is pragmatic and able to apply past experiences to problems. He searches for simple yet workable solutions, and is able to face difficulty with realism. He is able to write and speak directly to the point. He tends not to procrastinate.

On the other hand, the ST learner's liabilities are that he may be inflexible and unable to adapt to change. He may be dogmatic and headstrong. He has a limited tolerance for ambiguity and thus may take action before he has considered all the consequences. The ST learner may oversimplify complex issues or fail to see the possibilities beyond the immediate facts. He is overly concerned about what is right or wrong so that he overlooks the gray areas where the truth tends to lurk. He distrusts those thing which can't be quickly verified by the senses. Furthermore, because of his task orientation, he may overlook the feelings of the people with whom he is working.

Arian's greatest learning strength tends to be his dependency on sensing.

Sensors want to collect information through their sense functions, i.e., what they can see, touch, hear, smell and taste. What they trust is what they can verify with their senses. As such, they tend to have a "here and now" preference for learning that is focused on questions of practicality, functionality, do-ability, drill, practice, repetition, skill development, usefulness, sequence, how to do it, and knowledge of what it's good for. Sensors make up 75 percent of public school student populations.

Learning Preferences

Arian's preferences for the Sensing Thinking and the Sensing Feeling learning styles are indicated by these choices:

Sensing Thinking First Choices:
- "I'm good at getting things done.
- When I'm making something I prefer to follow the directions one step at a time.
- I would like to be in business, politics or construction.
- When I have a difficult assignment I like to memorize or practice what needs to be done.
- I enjoy doing things I know about and can do well.
- I prefer games that are fast and have lots of action and where someone wins.
- I would like to make a lot of money.
- In school the most important thing to me is getting good grades.
- When I have a problem I like to work it out step by step.
- When I have many assignments to do I start working right away and finish one assignment before beginning another.
- I like assignments that I know I can do well.
- I am at my best when knowing exactly what to do.
- I like to make something I can use.
- I prefer assignments that I can do quickly and well.
- I prefer to learn by answering questions in a workbook or on worksheets.
- I learn best when I can apply skills I have already learned or memorized.

Sensing Feeling First Choices:
- I like questions that ask me how I feel about things.
- I work best when I'm having fun.
- I like assignments or activities that involve sharing my feelings and ideas.
- I like books about people's feelings and personal problems.
- My best ideas come from talking with people.

Sensing Thinking Preferred Learning Environment

The ST learner learns best in an organized, systematic, activity-oriented, instructor-directed atmosphere. He needs to be actively engaged in purposeful work., The instructional environment requires well-defined procedures and content. This content needs to be presented in an orderly and systematic manner. The instructional emphases for the ST are on competitive and independent approaches to learning.

The ST learns best when he can directly experience with his five senses what he is expected to learn. Motivation comes from being able to see the practicality of what he has learned and putting the new learning into immediate use. Thus, the ST learns best when he can see the utility of what he is being asked to learn.

The ST learner has little tolerance for ambiguous situations. He wants to know what is expected of him before he begins. He needs well stated ground rules. He works best when there are clearly stated objectives, and when achievement is quickly recognized and rewarded. The ST learner likes games that are competitive, have clear rules, and have lots of action.

The ST learner needs a well defined instructional approach with the focus on content mastery or the mastery of basic skills. He benefits from an immediate opportunity to employ what has been learned.

The Sensing Thinking Learner Learns Best From:

- Repetition drill
- Memorization
- Programmed instruction
- Workbooks
- Demonstration
- Trips
- Direct actual experience

Motivating Activities That Most Support the ST Learner:

- Practice
- Mastery Learning
- Convergent Thinking tasks
- Direct actual experience
- Simple repetitive learning games
- Concrete exploration and manipulation
- Programmed Texts
- Making real-life models
- Reading biographies and How-To-Do-It books
- Dramatizing important events
- Making things that he can use in school, at home, and at play
- Demonstrating what he knows
- Assignments that have a clearly defined conclusion

Characteristics of the Extrovert

The extrovert focuses his energies on the external world of ideas and objects. He is primarily influenced by his surroundings including people, things and phenomena. The extrovert tends to be objective. He tends to be more outgoing, more at ease in groups, and is willing to explore new interests and activities. The extrovert also tends to be more verbal and more socially aggressive.

The Extrovert:

- Likes variety and action
- Prefers to talk
- Is eager to share feelings and information
- Acts quickly to new situations
- Tends to be impatient with long-term tasks
- Doesn't seem to mind interruptions
- Likes to perform for others

Styles Needing Development

Arian's undeveloped capacities are the Intuitive Feeling and the Intuitive Thinking learning styles. The tasks requiring the most compensating behaviors are indicated by these choices:

Intuitive Feeling Fourth Choices:

- I'm good at discovering things.

- I like questions that ask me to think of new and original ideas.

- I would like to be in music or painting or writing.

- I like assignments or activities that involve taking ideas and changing them into something new and different.

- When I have a difficult assignment I like to find new and different ways of doing the assignment.

- In school the most important thing to me is using my ideas and my imagination.

- When I have a problem I like to find a new way to solve it.

- I am at my best when making up my own ideas.

- I prefer to learn by doing an original project.

- I learn best when I can do projects of my own choosing.

Intuitive Thinking Fourth Choices:

- I work best when I'm finding a solution to a problem.

- I enjoy reading about things that interest me.

- I prefer games that make me think about what to do (chess, Stratego, etc.)

- I would like to invent or discover something.

- I would like a job where I can read and think.

- When I have many assignments to do I think carefully about what needs to be done and then plan how best to do it.

- I like to investigate ideas.

- My best ideas come from reading about things.

Please refer to the section *Helping Students Develop Their Undeveloped Abilities* starting on page 49 in the LIP User's Manual for more information.

Post Script

Succeeding manuals in this series on "Dealing With Diversity" will address the preparation of curriculum, identification of pupil learning styles, identification of teaching styles, and management of the T.L.C. process. Each manual builds upon its predecessors. All manuals are addressed to assisting teachers and pupils in the movement toward confluence.

A pupil diagnostic test for preferred learning styles is also available in kit form. The kit contains 30 Learning Preference Inventories, 30 student folders, one Learning Style Inventory, one Teaching Style Inventory, and a User's Manual. An instrument is also available for administrators and project managers. This instrument, the Management Style Inventory, relates management styles to the Jungian behaviors by style.

Notes

Notes

Notes

Additional Materials

Silver Strong and Associates is the recognized leader in combining educational theory with practical classroom techniques, and has been publishing and consulting for the educational community for more than twenty-five years. Below are some of our most popular products—products designed to help teachers, administrators, and students be the best they can be.

The Learning Preference Inventory

The Most Reliable and Valid Instrument for Assessing Students' Learning Styles and Profiles

The Learning Preference Inventory (LPI) unlocks the door to improved learning by providing you with the information you need to select activities consistent with your students' interests and strengths. The LPI is one of the most valid and reliable instruments for assessing student learning styles and profiles. The 144 item instrument is based on the research of the Swiss psychiatrist C. G. Jung and his theory of personality type. It has an international reputation as one of the premiere learning style instruments and has been presented at the American Education Research Association. The inventory identifies student preferences for perception (sensing and intuition), processing (thinking and feeling), and participation (introversion and extroversion). The instrument is computer-scored and easy to administer. It is appropriate for grades 3 and higher.

The LPI has been used to:

- Assess student learning styles & profiles
- Diagnose and prescribe learning activities
- Work effectively with "at- risk" students
- Provide career counseling for school-to-work transition programs
- Identify students with special needs
- Select students for gifted programs
- Show parents how they can help their child learn best
- Conduct research studies

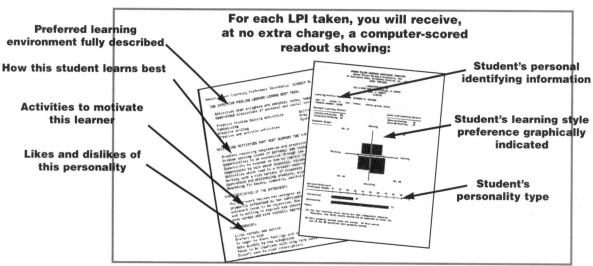

Preferred learning environment fully described

How this student learns best

Activities to motivate this learner

Likes and dislikes of this personality

For each LPI taken, you will receive, at no extra charge, a computer-scored readout showing:

Student's personal identifying information

Student's learning style preference graphically indicated

Student's personality type

Call **1-800-962-4432** for information and pricing or visit us on-line at **www.silverstrong.com**

The Unity in Diversity Series:

A critical resource for addressing the varying interests, needs, and learning styles found in today's classrooms

We live and learn in an increasingly diverse world. More and more, the American classroom reflects this reality. New students, new cultures, and new curricula appear daily, fueling the movement to address all forms of diversity – intellectual, physical, cultural, etc. The *Unity in Diversity Series* provides teachers, administrators, and curriculum directors with concrete strategies to motivate and cultivate learning in the complex world of today's classrooms. The series addresses the question, "How are all minds alike yet different?" and attempts to reconcile the often conflicting notions of unity and plurality.

TEACHING STYLES AND STRATEGIES

Transform your teaching into a true learning experience for everyone. This manual not only increases your repertoire of teaching strategies, your teaching confidence, and your awareness, it also enables you to help students become more responsible, autonomous learners. The eighteen tangible teaching strategies (arranged by learning style) help you design classroom lessons and staff development programs that will make excellence a reality for every teacher and student.

QUESTIONING STYLES AND STRATEGIES

The questions that we ask and the ways in which we ask them inevitably affect a child's success both in and out of the classroom. This manual provides you with more than thirty questioning strategies designed to actively engage students' minds and encourage them to think in a variety of ways.

NEW!

Tools For Promoting Active, In-Depth Learning

Transform Your Classroom Into An Aerobic Session For The Mind!

Tools for Promoting Active, In-Depth Learning provides every teacher with sixty classroom-tested, immediately-applicable techniques for actively engaging students in meaningful learning. By incorporating these effective tools or "moves" into your teaching, you can make active, in-depth learning a reality for every student now!

This indispensable manual includes:

- *An introduction to active, in-depth learning*
- *Over 60 practical tools for use in all subject areas and at all grade levels, including:*

  - *Tools for Generating, Visualizing, and Presenting Ideas*
  - *Tools for Focusing and Making Decisions*
  - *Tools for Writing and Reflection*
  - *Tools for Remembering, Reviewing, and Questioning*
  - *Tools for Promoting Cooperation*
  - *Tools for Assessing and Energizing Learning*

Call **1-800-962-4432** for information and pricing or visit us on-line at **www.silverstrong.com**

DIAGNOSTIC BEHAVIOR CHECKLIST

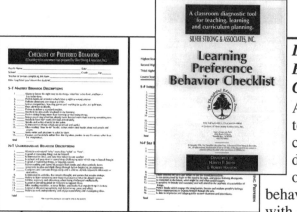

DIAGNOSTIC BEHAVIOR CHECKLIST
An observation tool (with a convenient folder design) that outlines 60 behaviors associated with each of the four learning styles. The checklist can be used to assess students at all grade levels (including pre-readers and ESL students).

Assessment Instruments for Adults

Self-knowledge is the key to personal growth and the realization of potentialities. At the same time, increased self-knowledge leads to a greater understanding of others. These instruments are for learners, teachers, coaches, and leaders who want to grow through self-knowledge and forge deeper, more meaningful relationships with students, peers, and staff.

The Learning Style Inventory for Adults (LSI)
The LSI is a self-scoring, 100-item inventory for identifying and graphically plotting your profile according to your dominant, auxiliary, tertiary, and least-used styles.

The Teaching Style Inventory (TSI)
This 56-item, self-diagnostic inventory will allow you to identify your teaching behaviors and decision-making processes in seven different capacities: planning, implementing, preferred environment, curriculum objectives, teaching objectives, teaching operations, classroom roles, and evaluation.

The Management Style Inventory (MSI)
The Athletic Coaching Style Inventory
These self-scoring inventories, designed specifically for administrators and coaches, will enable you to assess your leadership and motivational practices and build stronger working relationships with players and staff.

Learn about our extensive line of style-based curriculum units
Call **1-800-962-4432** for information and pricing
or visit us on-line at **www.silverstrong.com**